£8.50

Time to Meet

MARCUS BRAYBROOKE

TIME
TO
MEET

Towards a Deeper Relationship
between Jews and Christians

SCM PRESS
London

TRINITY PRESS INTERNATIONAL
Philadelphia

296.9

First published 1990

SCM Press Ltd
26–30 Tottenham Road
London N1 4BZ

Trinity Press International
3725 Chestnut Street
Philadelphia, Pa. 19104

© Marcus Braybrooke 1990

British Library Cataloguing in Publication Data

Braybrooke, Marcus
  Time to meet.
  1. Christian church. Relations with Judaism   2. Judaism.
  Relations with christian church
  I. Title
  261.26

  ISBN 0–334–02447–1

Library of Congress Cataloguing-in-Publication Data

Braybrooke, Marcus.
  Time to meet : towards a deeper relationship between Jews and
Christians / Marcus Braybrooke
    p.   cm
  Includes bibliographical references.
  ISBN 0–334–02447–1
  1. Judaism – Relations – Christianity – 1945– 2. Christianity and
other religions – Judaism – 1945– 3. Judaism (Christian theology)
I. Title
BM535.B675   1990
261.2′6–dc20   90–30880

Photoset at The Spartan Press Ltd, Lymington, Hants
and printed in Great Britain by
Richard Clay Ltd, Bungay, Suffolk

Contents

Contents

To George Appleton and Edward Carpenter
for their inspiration and friendship

To Sigmund Sternberg and Sidney Corob
for their generosity

Preface

I am grateful to members of the Council of Christians and Jews, the World Congress of Faiths, other inter-faith groups and the congregation of Christ Church, Bath, with whom I have shared my ideas and whose comments and questions have shaped my thinking. Most of the material in this book began as talks, and some of it, at different stages of development, has appeared in print.

Some of chapters 5 and 6 appeared in a Modern Churchpeople's Union pamphlet, *Jews and Christians: Can Jesus draw us together?*, and some of the material was also used in a paper that I presented to the Council of World Religions Conference in Turkey in May 1988. Some of the material on 'Praying Together' appeared in *Dialogue and Alliance*, Spring 1989, Vol. 3, No. 1, and the material on the Holocaust was first prepared for a paper presented to the 1988 Oxford Conference on the Holocaust. I have used some of the material in the chapters on 'God and Father of Us All' and 'Shared Responsibility' in an essay for a book on 'Nationhood' to be published by the British Council of Churches and in *The Violent Society*, ed. Eric Moonman, Frank Cass and Co 1987. The material on statements by the churches was first prepared for the Irish Council of Christians and Jews for a lecture given in Dublin and the discussion of the covenant for a paper given to the Hebrew Christian Alliance.

I am also grateful for the unfailing encouragement and constructive criticism of Dr John Bowden, Editor of SCM Press, and to Rabbi Tony Bayfield, and Tom and Fifi Charrington, who read the script and who made helpful suggestions and David Kessler for comments on 'Israel'. I also wish to thank my wife Mary, our son,

Jeremy, and our daughter and son-in-law, Rachel and Peter, for their comments and enthusiastic interest in my work for inter-faith and Christian–Jewish friendship.

November 1989   Marcus Braybrooke

Introduction

Twenty-five years of interfaith encounter have profoundly re-moulded my understanding of the Christian faith. Here I share primarily the particular impact of contact with Jews and Judaism. My hope is that this will help other Christians to rethink their faith, conscious of the Jewish reality.

Part One outlines, with some critical comments, the 'official' teaching of the churches, as expressed in the statements of representative bodies. These statements are familiar enough to specialists but still not widely known amongst church members. They provide the context for my personal attempt, in Part Two, to explore further the issues which now need to be tackled. The statements show that quite a lot has been done in recent years to purge Christian teaching of prejudice and anti-Judaism. Yet the rethinking and reformulation of the Christian faith demanded by a real appreciation of Judaism has scarcely begun. A new image is not enough. A profound inner change is required.[1]

The growing opposition to interfaith dialogue in some parts of the church is because opponents see it as questioning the faith 'once delivered to the saints'. Perhaps they are more aware of the demands of dialogue than some of its exponents. As dialogue has become more fashionable, the radical nature of its call to leave the shell of tradition and take the risk of 'unprotected living'[2] is in danger of being blunted.

Faith, for me, involves a constant search for a deeper awareness of the Divine Mystery, not a holding on to fixed doctrines. In that search today, if we will, we may be illuminated by the insights of all the great spiritual traditions. I do not suggest that religions all say the same thing: but each, with its particular view, is a window on to the divine. As we overcome past bitterness and learn to share what we see, we may hope to grow in understanding of each other, to be enriched in our awareness of God's glory and to be inspired in common service of a divided and needy world. This is why the inter-faith movement has rightly been called a 'pilgrimage of hope'. A growing number of Christians have embarked on this journey. I shall be glad if this book encourages others to set out, and in particular if it helps the churches to grapple seriously with the profound rethinking of the Christian faith which an awareness of Jews and Judaism requires. The Christian relationship to Judaism is central to Christianity's own self-understanding, which has often been marred by a perverted view of Judaism.

'The exterior dialogue must always be matched by the interior dialogue.' These words of Fr Murray Rogers, an Anglican pioneer of spiritual dialogue, whom I visited at his ashram when I first went to India, have stayed with me.[3] To be open to those of other faiths is to be open to change, although as Teilhard de Chardin once said, it is possible to travel round the world and not move an inch.

After a conversation with a person of another faith, I find myself engaged in an interior conversation and in prayer as I seek to interpret and assimilate what I have talked about with the other. It is not a matter of accommodating beliefs, as critics sometimes suggest, so as to smoothe away differences, but a life process of reflection on the beliefs I already have in the light of wider understanding and of different approaches to the divine.[4] Others may ask questions which encourage me to think out more fully beliefs which I had largely taken for granted. I was surprised when a Hindu, quite seriously, said he had not realized that Christians taught monogamy – but then, if his picture of Christendom was derived from Hollywood, he might well have been misled!

This process has been described as 'passing over' by John Dunne, an American professor of religious studies, in his book *The Way of All the Earth*. 'Passing over,' he writes, 'is a shifting of standpoint, a going over to the standpoint of another culture, another way of life, another religion. It is followed by an equal and opposite process we might call "coming back", coming back with new insight to one's own culture, one's own way of life, one's own religion.'[5] There are moments when one is inclined to linger and try to identify completely with the new culture, and for some people this is their chosen path, but I have always been conscious that it was as a follower of Jesus that I was welcomed as a guest by those of other faiths.

My first exposure was to Hinduism. At Madras Christian College and Madras University I studied Hindu philosophy and the devotional religion of the Tamils. I also stayed with several brahmins in their homes.

After the linguistic philosophy of Cambridge, which questioned whether it was possible even to talk of God, the Hindu philosophical acceptance of mystical or intuitive knowledge of God was refreshing. The emphasis on the mystical, as the great nineteenth-century Hindu seer Sri Ramakrishna taught, suggested an underlying unity of religions in their experience of the divine, even if their formulations of that experience were very different.

Then, back in Britain, as a member of the World Congress of Faiths, my circle of friends began to include members of all religions. Because they were themselves interested in inter-religious understanding, they were often criticized by members of their own religion and were critical of the conservatism which characterizes every religion. Amongst these friends were a number of Jews deeply committed to interfaith fellowship and co-operation.

In 1977 I spent three months at the Ecumenical Institute for Theological Study at Tantur, Jerusalem. There I learned more about the Jewish milieu of the life and ministry of Jesus. His historicity and humanity became more real, as I walked in the Judaean hills or by the sea of Galilee. The Psalms, especially with their frequent references to the elements, became more vivid, and I realized that their repeated affirmation of God's loving kindness came from the heart of Jewish faith. I also met with those working for understanding between the various religious communities in Israel. Slowly I began to sense how deeply many Jews and Arabs, both Muslim and Christian, had been hurt and how essential is forgiveness, but how costly. I became more aware of the difficulty and cost of interfaith dialogue, but also of its urgent necessity. As Pope John Paul II said to a delegation of the International Council of Christians and Jews, 'Dialogue is an apparently modest, but in the end very effective way to peace.'[6] I realized, too, although I had often preached about forgiveness, that I had not experienced the depth of anguish suffered by so many in that land nor recognized how painful and demanding it is to forgive when one has been severely wounded.

In 1984, to my surprise, I was asked to become Executive Director of the Council of Christians and Jews. CCJ is the national organization in Britain which encourages understanding between Jews and Christians and which brings them together in the struggle against prejudice and discrimination. Through the International Council of Christians and Jews (ICCJ), it is linked with similar bodies in other countries, such as the National Conference of Christians and Jews (NCCJ) in the USA.

I very quickly discovered that not everyone wishes the dialogue enterprise well. There are evangelical Christian groups, often based in or financed from the USA, who actively seek the conversion of Jews to Christianity and see dialogue as dangerously misleading. There are Jews who hope to strengthen group identity and commitment by seeing themselves surrounded by a hostile and marauding church. There are antisemites, posing perhaps as virulent anti-Zionists, who foment disharmony.

I soon discovered also how many Christians and Jews had devotedly given of their time, energy and scholarship to help build a new relationship between Jews and Christians. The positive developments are most encouraging, but too little known outside the circle of scholars and those hooked on dialogue. Even amongst scholars, because of their specialisms, the wider implications of the new relationship are not always recognized. The more also that I studied church statements, the more I felt that they were often a diplomatic evasion of the issues.

The new understanding of the relationship of Jews and Christians should raise searching questions for Christians about their self-understanding of their faith. Christians need to face these issues so that improved relations with Jews are made secure. There is now much goodwill towards Jews in the Christian churches, but without far-reaching theological changes within the churches, this goodwill has a flimsy basis. Very easily affirmation of Christ carries anti-Jewish implications, whilst claims for the 'universal Gospel' belittle Judaism and encourage missionary effort. Many involved in Christian–Jewish relations seek quick results, but the changes required will take time. They need theological reflection and they need to permeate most areas of theological study.

This reflection is also, I believe, important for Christians' own understanding of their faith – for 'interior' dialogue – and indeed for the very integrity of the faith. It can help Christians come to a more vivid picture of Jesus in his historical setting. It can help Christians rethink christology, as they consider what the titles of Jesus meant to the Jews who first used them. It can help to purge the churches of their triumphalism, as they become penitently aware of their share of responsibility for Jewish sufferings through the centuries. It can help us all come to a deeper understanding of human nature and of the mystery of a God of love whose presence we affirm, even in the midst of great evil and suffering.

In this book, I reflect on how my understanding of Christianity has changed as a result of learning more about Judaism and of talking with many Jews and Christians engaged in this dialogue. I hope it will serve as an introduction to more specialist studies, especially for readers in Britain, as so much of the literature has been published either in the USA or on the European continent. Even more important, I hope it will prod the churches towards the rethinking and reformulating of the Christian faith which seems to me essential if the new relationship between Jews and Christians is to be securely established.

Yet if these reflections have any lasting validity it will be because they point towards a more authentic understanding of the Christian faith. For a Christian's first loyalty is to the truth as he or she understands it. Good relations may flow from agreement about the truth, but dialogue at its deepest is always a search for truth – it is not a matter of compromise or religious negotiation.

Visiting Israel made me aware that Jesus was a Jew, but I still thought of him as one in opposition to the religious leaders of his day. I have come to see that he should be understood as a 'faithful son of the covenant'. Otherwise, we look for a way in which he was different to or superior to the Judaism in which he was nurtured. We are then tempted to perpetuate mistaken understandings of Judaism as a 'religion of law' and to continue the misrepresentation of Pharisaism. Jesus was a faithful Jew. His significance cannot honestly be affirmed by pointing to ways in which he was different from the Judaism of his time, which has so often been unfairly depicted. We have instead to be able to make sense of his life and ministry within a Jewish setting and yet explain the parting of the ways and how a new religion emerged. The difference seems to lie in Jesus' expectation that the new age was dawning. For his first disciples this was confirmed in the resurrection experience. Other Jews, equally devout, saw no evidence that redemption was at hand. The continuing Jewish 'no' to Jesus may be a warning to Christians not so to spiritualize salvation that they forget the urgent need to redeem the world from violence, poverty and injustice.

Those who did first believe in Jesus were Jewish. The terms in which they spoke of him were drawn from the Jewish scriptures. It seems that when such terms as 'Son' or 'Lord' were taken over by an increasingly Gentile church, they acquired an altered meaning. The credal formulations of the church councils, emphasizing that Christ was 'very God', aggravated the gap between church and synagogue. Too often the affirmation that 'Christ is Lord' has carried with it implicit anti-Judaism. But are we bound by those formulations or are we able to affirm that God was in Christ in a way which unites us with his own people?

This may be made possible by the increasing recognition that God has not rejected his covenant with his people Israel. The old covenant is not abrogated by the new. What then is the relationship of the two covenants? Does the new covenant merely extend the promises of the old to the Gentiles? But there are different values enshrined in the two religions and some Jews convert to Christianity and some Christians become Jews. Further, instead of Christian exclusivism, sometimes it seems a new Jewish–Christian exclusivism is being constructed that has no place for the other great world religious traditions. My own view is that Christians need to recognize God's saving activity within *all* the great religious traditions. In affirming that God is present in Christ, we can also affirm that God is present in the Torah, the Qur'an and in the teachings of the East. I would echo the words of Dr Rosen, the former Chief Rabbi of Ireland, that 'the deepening of dialogue implies a diversity of paths to God and is a process of religious growth and enrichment by which we become all the more aware of the Divine Omnipresence in its unlimited diversity'.[7]

Quite a number of Christians do not accept such a view. The attempt to build a new relationship between Jews and Christians is seriously hampered by the continuing efforts of some Christians to convert Jews. Whilst Christians continue actively trying to convert Jews to Christianity, they imply that the new covenant is superior to the old and create the suspicion that dialogue is a change of tactic rather than a change of heart. Yet some of my most interesting conversations with rabbis have been about Jesus. For where there is openness and trust, it is natural to share our deepest convictions. As

David Sheppard, Bishop of Liverpool, has said, 'I do not believe that respect for the other person means we should avoid ever speaking of our own faith. True respect will include sharing the most precious things of our faith if there comes an appropriate moment. It will also include opening ourselves to want to listen to the precious things of the other's faith.'[8] Any hint of conversionism destroys trust.

Over all such dialogue with Jews, the Shoah or Holocaust, of course, casts its long and ugly shadow. Not a day passed at the Council of Christians and Jews without some reminder of it. Even so, the horror of the Shoah is something I scarcely feel I have begun to fathom, however much I read or see. The Christian has to try to come to terms with the church's share of responsibility for Jewish suffering, both because of its failure vigorously enough to oppose Hitler and because of its long centuries of anti-Jewish teaching. Deep penitence is essential together with unlearning the anti-Judaism that pervades Christian teaching, liturgy and practice. The challenge is put like this by the Jewish theologian Marc Ellis, who has attempted to construct a Jewish theology of liberation: 'Only by entering into the nothingness of the death camps can a contemporary Christian way of life become authentic.'[9] To do this, Christians need Jewish help.[10] 'We Christians can never go back behind Auschwitz; to go beyond Auschwitz is impossible for us by ourselves. It is possible only together with the victims of Auschwitz,' says the German Catholic theologian, Johannes Baptist Metz.[11]

The Shoah, however, poses deep questions to all people of faith, which Jew and Christian are beginning to grapple with together. What is now our understanding of human nature, knowing as we do the bestial potential within each one of us? How too do we affirm a God of love after Auschwitz? Many traditional pictures of God's power to intervene or over-rule no longer seem satisfactory. Indeed such pictures of divine male power, which do not allow for freedom and variety, may underlie the domineering attitudes that many Christians have shown not only to Jews but also to women, to people of other races and cultures and indeed to the animal creation.[12] Increasingly I sense that God's only power is the demand of suffering love, embodied by Jesus Christ. God makes himself one with those who suffer to appeal through them to the conscience of the world.

As a pacifist and aware of God's presence with the poor and suffering, I have found the question of Israel intensely difficult. Whatever is said may add to the sufferings of others. The horrors of the Shoah make me question whether pacifism is an adequate response to evil. I can understand that after centuries of being without power and at the mercy of others, many Jews speak of 'empowerment' and stress the need of strength for security and for life itself. No one should prescribe non-violence for others, but the way of non-violence remains for me integral to the following of Jesus – not that this has been the dominant Christian tradition. Armed force may buy time and hold evil in check. It cannot root out hostility nor reconcile enmity.

Christian–Jewish dialogue is all too easily liable to be hijacked by events in Israel. A Christian has to understand that the existence of Israel is integral to the self-understanding of almost all Jews. A Christian should also seek to enter into the real fear and insecurity of many Israelis. Often it must seem that Christians are quick to criticize, before they have convinced Jews of their total commitment to Israel's right to exist. I may be critical of a relation, but I will defend him or her as a member of the family against outside criticism. I doubt, however, whether many Christians are felt by Jews to be 'members of the family'. Any criticism is heard as coming from outside and it may be particularly resented if it appears that Christians are adopting a position of moral superiority.

There is, however, legitimate criticism of the policies and actions of particular Israeli governments (as of all governments) and Jews certainly indulge in this.[13] A concern for human rights should be universal. This should be the basis for criticism and this is why it is important for Jews, Christians and Muslims to speak and act together on issues of human rights and to criticize all governments for violations of human rights. The criticism is not of Jew by Christian nor of Christian by Muslim, but on the basis of our common humanity. To plead for justice for the Palestinians is, I believe, also in the long term interest of Israel and the health of her democracy.[14]

In my view, the greatest contribution outsiders can make is to listen, but as they hear of the pain people have suffered they should gently avoid reinforcing it, but help those who have been hurt to recognize that others have been hurt as well. All have suffered injustice, all have been hurt and a new beginning is only possible when that hurt can be accepted and people are willing to make themselves vulnerable to others. The outsider can only pray and plead for honesty, for justice and for mutual reconciliation.

The existence of Israel also raises important questions about the Land and about the relationship of religion to society and politics. Recently there has been growing discussion between Jewish and Christian leaders about moral and practical issues on which they can speak and act together. Although it is at once apparent that neither community is agreed within itself on many of these matters, this concern ensures that dialogue does not become introverted. The coming together of religions is not for their own sake but for the good of the world. My deep conviction is that only together can the religions of the world offer the spiritual resources necessary to ensure a just and peaceful future for the world, which modern technology has made one. Together they should make their contribution to global survival.

At its deepest, meeting with those of other faiths not only leads to internal dialogue in which we rethink our understanding of our beliefs and our behaviour. It may become a means of spiritual growth and a religious experience. There is a risk, which involves a willingness to let go old certainties. But we discover that, although our understanding may be shaken, the reality of God's presence upholding us may become more real. We may also, as we share at a spiritual level with those of other faiths, find a oneness in God's presence which is deeper than any words.

The possibility of being together in prayer and waiting on God seems to some disloyalty or superficial mixing of faiths. To those who share in the voyage of discovery to which the interfaith pilgrimage invites us, it is a symbol of the new reality that we have discovered. God is present in all communities of faith. The new relationship that is being built between Jews and Christians is a sign of hope to all people.

It has been said that when peace comes to Jerusalem, peace will come to the whole world. Equally, if after centuries of tragic division Jews and Christians are being reconciled, then we may hope that reconciliation is possible amongst others who are deeply divided. The lessons learned in the search for Christian–Jewish understanding are significant for other areas of conflict. These lessons include the need for honesty to recognize and confess past prejudice and a willingness to rethink inherited teaching. Whether the churches are able to admit past error and affirm their faith without belittling the beliefs of others, makes their relationship to Judaism a touchstone of their integrity. If they are, then we can perhaps picture a day when the religions of the world start to contribute to a global theology and spirituality. In this the variety of our approaches to the divine do not threaten human unity but together enrich our awareness of the One who is 'beyond all names'.[15]

PART ONE

What are the Churches Saying?

1

Roman Catholic Statements

'The official theology of Christian churches is not determined by theologians or the common belief of Christians but by decisions taken at synods, conventions, and assemblies by delegates chosen to represent the membership at large, including theologians.'[1] Church statements serve as a touchstone. They will lag behind the thinking of the pioneers of a new Christian–Jewish relationship, but they will be ahead of the teaching in the average local church.

In this chapter, we shall consider the statements of the Roman Catholic Church, concentrating on the Second Vatican Council decrees *Nostra Aetate* (1965) and the two Vatican documents, issued on the tenth and twentieth anniversaries of *Nostra Aetate*, known as *Guidelines* (1975) and *Notes* (1985).

Nostra aetate

The decree *Nostra Aetate*, promulgated in October 1965 by the Second Vatican Council, was a decisive turning point in Catholic–Jewish relations. Although there was bitter controversy surrounding earlier drafts of the resolution, *Nostra Aetate* turned its back on centuries of hostility. It did not, however, recognize Christian responsibility for Jewish suffering nor did it mention the Holocaust nor the existence of the state of Israel. That Vatican II did address the subject of Catholic–Jewish relations was largely due to the personal concern of Pope John XXIII who, whilst Papal Nuncio at Istanbul, had made baptismal certificates available to Jews to save them from the Nazis.

In preparation for the Council, the hierarchy in 134 countries was asked to suggest agenda items. Antisemitism was one matter put forward, especially from the USA. The task of preparing state-

ments on this subject was entrusted to the Secretariat for the
Promotion of Christian Unity, under Cardinal Bea SJ.

It proved to be a long and tortuous path that he had to tread
before a statement was eventually adopted. Towards the end of
Session One, to counter rumours, assurances were given that the
issue would indeed be addressed. During the second session, when
delay again seemed likely, the draft statement was leaked to the
New York Times. The draft said it was wrong to accuse the Jewish
people 'either of Jesus' time or of today' of deicide. There was no
note of regret for past errors of the church and it was unclear
whether the Jewish people of today were considered to have a
continuing place in God's purposes. In presenting the schema
Cardinal Bea stressed 'that there was no national or political
question. Especially there is no question of acknowledging the State
of Israel on the part of the Holy See.'[2] He stressed that the
statement was required because of the violent criminal antisemitism
of the Nazis, but to Jewish disappointment denied that antisemitism
arose from Catholic teaching. Rabbi Arthur Gilbert, who worked
for a time with the Jewish Reconstructionist Foundation and on the
staff of NCCJ, in his account of *The Vatican Council and the Jews*
writes: 'Twice Bea had failed to acknowledge any Christian roots
for, or complicity in, the anti-Semitism appearing in Western
civilization. At no time did he express any remorse at Jewish
sufferings in the past or make any admission of Christian error . . .
In the end it seemed as though the Church was about "to forgive"
the Jews, when in fact most Jews felt it ought to be the Church that
sought forgiveness' (p. 97). Rabbi Lamm, in the official organ of
the Union of Orthodox Jewish Congregations of America, voiced
typical Jewish reactions. 'As Jews we object to being absolved of the
guilt of killing their God. To be absolved implies that one is guilty
but that nevertheless he is being forgiven. But we Jews never were
guilty and we do not therefore beg forgiveness . . . To our mind the
question is who will absolve the Church for its guilt in inspiring and
sponsoring crusades and inquisitions and blood libels and
pogroms . . . the Church has expressed to the Jewish people
neither apology nor confession nor regrets.'[3]

As a result of delaying tactics, the statement was not put to a vote.
Between sessions two and three, several events further complicated
the situation. First, Pope Paul VI, who had succeeded Pope John,
made a historic pilgrimage to the Holy Land, but continued to make

clear that the Vatican did not recognise Israel. As he was leaving, he defended Pope Pius XII, whose record had recently been attacked in the play, *The Deputy*, which had been written by a young German Protestant called Rolf Hochhuth. Secondly, there was deep conflict within the Jewish community about whether it was worth pursuing dialogue with the Catholic church. As a result of this, Orthodox Jews made clear that they would not engage in any 'theological' dialogue. This decision, which still holds, has had a continuing importance. Whilst co-operation on social problems was possible, Rabbi Soloveitchik, an acknowledged leader of the American Orthodox Jewish community, explained the impossibility of theological dialogue. 'The language of faith of a particular community is totally incomprehensible to the man of a different faith community. Hence, the confrontation should occur not at a theological, but at a mundane human level . . . The great encounter between man and God is a holy, personal and private affair, incomprehensible to the outsider . . . Each community is engaged in a singular gesture reflecting the nature of the act of faith itself and it is futile to try to find common denominators.'[4]

In response to the various complications, American Catholic bishops went out of their way to reassure Jewish audiences that a statement would be issued. But soon rumours started circulating that a weaker text had been drafted. The new statement, writes Rabbi Gilbert, 'refrained from absolving *Jews of the past* from a collective responsibility for the Crucifixion. It placed discussion of the relationship to the Jews within the context of hope for their eventual "entrance . . . into the fullness of the people of God established by Christ", a union awaited "with great desire". It avoided any mention of Christian involvement in past Jewish suffering. It failed to reassert Christian convictions concerning the reconciling significance of the Crucifixion. While it defined the Church as "the continuation of that people with which at one time God, in His ineffable mercy, desired to conclude the ancient pact . . .", it dealt not at all with the contemporaneous significance of the Jewish people' (p. 147). The draft did strongly condemn hatred and persecution of the Jews and said that the Jews of today should not be described as an accursed people.

Many American Catholic bishops worked for a stronger statement, which eventually was drafted. This was now placed as part of the 'Declaration on the Relationship of the Church to non-Christian

Religions'. It was accepted, in outline, towards the end of the third
session. Before the fourth and final session, the Pope ordered a
further revision of the Good Friday prayers, but any Jewish
goodwill that this might have occasioned was destroyed when, in an
extempore address, he spoke of the Jews killing Jesus. Once again
also rumours started to circulate – this time to the effect that
reference to 'deicide' was to be dropped.

The final statement was itself part of a wider declaration on non-
Christian religions. The statement showed an epoch-making
openness, although perhaps the special relationship of the church to
the Jewish people may have been obscured. Detailed changes tried
to placate the opposition. The bond was described as 'spiritual'.
From the sentence 'the Church of Christ acknowledges . . . that the
beginnings of her faith are found among the Hebrew patriarchs and
prophets', the phrase 'with a grateful heart' was dropped, 'lest it be
understood as if we had to give thanks to the Jews of today'.
Judaism was defined as a religion preparing for Christianity. The
Jews were no longer regarded as God's people. Jewish opposition to
Jesus was emphasized and it was said that Jewish authorities and
those who followed them pressed for the death of Christ. Specific
reference to 'deicide' was omitted. On the other hand, condemnation of antisemitism was strengthened.[5]

Soon after the Council, Cardinal Bea issued *Civiltà Cattolica*.
This was a summary of the Catholic Church's teachings on 'the role
of the Jewish people in the Divine plan of salvation'.[6] In twenty-
eight packed pages, he contrasted the formulations of the Council
with traditional teachings.

Whilst in retrospect the weaknesses of *Nostra Aetate* are evident,
it has in fact proved the basis for building a new relationship. The
section on the Jewish religion begins by recalling the spiritual bond
that links the people of the New Covenant to Abraham's stock and
affirms God's continuing covenant with the Jewish people. 'God
holds the Jews most dear for the sake of their Fathers; He does not
repent of the gifts He makes or of the calls he issues.'[7] The
document commends dialogue. 'This Sacred Synod wants to foster
and recommend that mutual understanding and respect which is the
fruit, above all, of biblical and theological studies as well as
fraternal dialogues' (p. 1). Most important, the charge of deicide is
repudiated, although the word is not used. 'True, the Jewish
authorities and those who followed their lead pressed for the death

of Christ; still, what happened in His passion cannot be charged against all the Jews, without distinction, then alive, nor against the Jews of today. Although the Church is the new people of God, the Jews should not be presented as rejected or accursed by God.' (p. 2). The decree also condemns all persecution and particularly displays of antisemitism.

Guidelines

Various national and provincial synods have sought to extend and apply the teaching of *Nostra Aetate*. Of particular importance are two documents emanating from the Vatican on the tenth and twentieth anniversaries of *Nostra Aetate*. In 1974 Pope Paul set up a Commission for Religious Relations with the Jews. In the following year, it produced *Guidelines and Suggestions for Implementing the Conciliar Declaration Nostra Aetate*.

Recognizing the spiritual bonds and historical links binding the church to Judaism and condemning antisemitism, the document stresses the need for Christians to understand Jews as 'they define themselves in the light of their own religious experience'.[8] The *Guidelines* commend dialogue, 'which demands respect for the other as he is; above all, respect for his faith and religious convictions' (p. 12). Acknowledging the church's divine mission to preach Jesus Christ, the church should take care that its witness does not give offence to Jews. There is an interesting encouragement to pray together. 'In whatever circumstances as shall prove possible and mutually acceptable, one might encourage a common meeting in the presence of God, in prayer and silent meditation, a highly efficacious way of finding that humility, that openness of heart and mind, necessary prerequisites for a deep knowledge of oneself and others. In particular that will be done in connection with great causes, such as the struggle for peace and justice' (p. 12).

Liturgical links are stressed and the need in commenting on biblical texts to emphasize 'the continuity of our faith with that of the earlier Covenant' (p. 13). There is a sensitive discussion of the problems of apparently anti-Jewish passages in the New Testament, such as St John's use of 'Jews'. The text itself cannot be altered, but in its liturgical use, 'there should be an overriding preoccupation to bring out explicitly the meaning of a text' (p. 13). It is suggested that 'the leaders of the Jews' or 'the adversaries of

Jesus' brings out John's meaning better than just the misleading term 'Jews'.

The section 'Teaching and Education' makes several important points. The same God inspires both Testaments; Judaism in the time of Christ was complex and varied; Judaism must not be presented as a 'religion of only justice, fear and legalism' (p. 14); Jesus was Jewish and his death must not be blamed on all Jews; and the history of Judaism did not end with the destruction of Jerusalem, but went on to develop a religious tradition, 'rich in religious values' (p. 15).

The importance of a new understanding of Judaism for all Christians is emphasized. 'The problem of Jewish–Christian relations concerns the Church as such, since it is when "pondering her own mystery" that she encounters the mystery of Israel. Therefore, even in areas where no Jewish communities exist, this remains an important problem' (p. 15).

Notes

To mark the twentieth anniversary of *Nostra Aetate*, the Commission for Religious Relations with the Jews published *Notes on the Correct Way to present Jews and Judaism in preaching and catechesis in the Roman Catholic Church*. The document, after recalling statements of the Holy Father, insists that because of the unique relationship between Christianity and Judaism, 'the Jews and Judaism should not occupy an occasional and marginal place in catechesis: their presence there is essential and should be organically integrated'.[9] It is not just a historical interest, but 'a *pastoral* concern for a still living reality . . . with "the people of God of the Old Covenant, which has never been revoked"' (p. 13).

The 'singular character and the difficulty of Christian teaching about Jews and Judaism' is seen to lie in the need to balance a number of pairs of ideas, such as 'Promise and Fulfilment'. This led to a passage about mission which caused some misunderstanding amongst Jews. 'The Church and Judaism cannot then be seen as two parallel ways of salvation and the Church must witness to Christ as the Redeemer for all, "while maintaining the strictest respect for religious liberty in line with the teaching of the Second Vatican Council (Declaration *Dignitatis Humanae*)"' (p. 13). In his press release, Mgr Jorge Mejia, Secretary of the Commission, added that the affirmation concerning the centrality of Christ and his unique value in the economy of salvation was 'important for the Catholic Church. . . . Clearly this does not mean, however, that the Jews cannot and should not draw salvific gifts from their own traditions. Of course, they can, and should do so' (p. 6).

The second section on 'The Relations between the Old and New Testament' aims to show the unity of biblical revelation. A footnote mentions that 'old' is not used in the sense of 'out-of-date' or 'outworn'. 'It is the permanent value of the Old Testament as a source of Christian Revelation that is emphasized here' (p. 13). The discussion of typology, which implies that the church reads the Old Testament in the light of Christ, seemed to some to return to a 'supersessionist' approach. The document itself admits that 'typology makes many people uneasy and is perhaps the sign of a problem unresolved' (p. 14). At the press conference given by Mgr Jorge Mejia, he said, 'It should also be noted that the limits of "typological" usage are acknowledged, and other possible ways of reading the Old Testament in relation to the New are not excluded' (p. 6).

The third section dealt with 'Jewish Roots of Christianity'. It begins by saying that 'Jesus was and always remained a Jew' (p. 15). In a commentary, Michel Remaud, a French priest, who studied Judaism at the University of Jerusalem, adds, 'First and foremost this means that Jesus is not a *convert*. He never abjured his Judaism, nor did he in any way disown his origins or his past. But this also means that the Risen Jesus remains a Jew' (p. 27). Jesus' submission to the law and his teaching in synagogues is noted. An important section makes clear that the relations with the Pharisees were not 'always or wholly polemical' and that Jesus shared many Pharisaic doctrines and used their method of interpreting scripture. 'It is noteworthy too that the Pharisees are not mentioned in accounts of the Passion' (p. 16).

The fourth section deals with 'The Jews in the New Testament'. Here it is recognized that the 'Gospels are the outcome of long and complicated editorial work . . . Hence it cannot be ruled out that some references hostile or less than favourable to the Jews have their historical context in conflicts between the nascent Church and the Jewish community. Certain controversies reflect Christian–Jewish relations long after the time of Jesus' (p. 16).

The fifth section deals with 'The Liturgy' and the final section with 'Judaism and Christianity in History'. Through the Diaspora, after the fall of Jerusalem in 70 CE, the Jewish people was able 'to carry to the whole world a witness – often heroic – of its fidelity to the one God . . . while preserving the memory of the land of their forebears at the heart of their hope' (p. 18). Eugene Fisher, who is a consultant to the Commission, comments: 'This statement is truly remarkable. Jewish "hope" had previously been defined – and its validity acknowledged – in an eschatological sense: "The people of God of the Old and the New Testaments are tending toward a like end in the future: *the coming or return* of the Messiah – even if they start from two different points of view . . . Thus it can be said that Jews and Christians meet in a *comparable* hope, founded on the same promise to Abraham." The Jewish "no" to Jesus as "the Christ" (Messiah) is here put in a larger, more positive framework: God's overall plan for humanity. Indeed, Christians can learn from this "no", this continuing Jewish witness in and for the world that "we must also accept our responsibility to prepare the world for the coming of the Messiah by working together for social justice . . . and international reconciliation"' (pp. 24f. nn. 10f.). Here there is a recognition of Judaism's continuing witness and that the Jewish 'no' to Jesus has a place in God's purposes.

The permanence of Israel, it is said, 'is a historic fact and a sign to be interpreted within God's design'. 'The existence of the State of Israel and its political options should be envisaged not in a perspective which is in itself religious, but in their reference to the common principles of international law' (p. 24). This caused some misunderstanding. Fr Mejia explained that Christians, by this section, were encouraged to try to understand the 'religious attachment' of the Jews to the 'land of their forefathers'. It also speaks of the creation of the State of Israel. Fr Mejia pointed out: 'It will surely be noted that for the first time in a document of this Commission, in different but related paragraphs, reference is made to the land and the state' (p. 7). With 'extreme precision', it is made clear that the state should be regarded in terms of international law and not from a religious perspective. As Eugene Fisher explains, this was a caution for Catholics against biblical fundamentalism. 'It is in no case a denial of the religious relationship of the Jewish people to "Eretz Israel", or of the validity or the necessity of the Jewish state, which it supports' (p. 26). Indeed reference is made to the 1975 USA Catholic Bishops declaration, which declared that Jews regarded themselves as 'a peoplehood that is not solely racial, ethnic or religious, but in a sense a composite of all these. It is for such reasons that an overwhelming majority of Jews see themselves bound in one way or another to the land of Israel. Most Jews see this tie to the land as essential to their Jewishness. Whatever difficulties Christians may experience in sharing this view, they should strive to understand this link between land and people which Jews have expressed in their writings and worship throughout two millennia as a longing for the homeland, holy Zion' (p. 25). It is clearly recognized that the land and state of Israel have a religious significance for the great majority of Jews, but this does not necessarily imply that the state of Israel has a religious significance for Christians. For them, it is a matter of 'international law'.

This section also recognizes 'the continuous spiritual fecundity of Judaism in the Middle Ages and in modern times' and makes the first reference in a Vatican document to the Holocaust. 'Catechesis should help in understanding the meaning for the Jews of the extermination during the years 1939–1945, and its consequences' (p. 18). The brevity of this reference is expanded by Mgr Mejia. 'A brief sentence at the end of the paragraph refers to the "extermination" of the Jews (in Hebrew, the *shoah* i.e. the catastrophe) during the dark years of the Nazi persecution. It calls upon Catholics to understand how decisive such a tragedy was for the Jews, a tragedy that is also obviously ours. Several teaching aids have been prepared, including those by Catholic offices for education, to help Catholics better comprehend the senseless dimensions of this tragedy and to grasp better its significance' (p. 7).

In Eugene Fisher's view, 'In some areas the "Notes" offer a clear and significant advance over earlier documents of the Holy See' (p. 24). The permanence of Israel and its continuous spiritual fecundity is recognized, as is the essential place of Judaism in catechesis. The relationship of Jesus with the Pharisees is put in a new light and the Holocaust is more clearly mentioned, as is the land and state of Israel. The document also begins to grapple with the theological significance of the Jewish 'no' to Jesus and hints at a positive response to 'the permanence of Israel' (pp. 20–3).

The critical reaction of many Jews to the document, however, was a reminder, in Fisher's words, that dialogue is still in its babyhood. 'Jews, reading the *Notes*, are surprised that Catholics in the main could not have predicted how Jews would react to key passages (e.g. on typology) and wonder, further, even once the text is explained, how Catholics could get themselves so lost in the intricacies of theological "balancing" . . . Part of this sense of surprise, I would surmise, stems from our differences of style. Catholicism works itself out, in practice, precisely through the intricacies of theological nuance, Judaism through the equal delicacies of *halachic* distinction . . . The key is trust. The very imperfections of the document . . . reveal the depth of the faith-substance with which the dialogue must yet deal . . . In such an effort, the presumption must always be in favour of the integrity of the other's intentions. Neither hasty press releases nor unconsulted promulgations will prove the best tools with which to build our bridges of trust . . . Judaism, no less than Christianity, comes from God. This was the central message of the Second Vatican Council, and one to which we Catholics must re-commit ourselves in each generation' (p. 26).

Catholic documents show enormous advances, but they show also, in the words of Eugene Fisher just quoted, 'the depth of the faith-substance with which the dialogue must yet deal'.

2

The World Council of Churches and Member Churches

1. The World Council of Churches

The World Council of Churches (WCC) brings together over 300 Protestant, Anglican, Orthodox (since 1961) and Pentecostal churches. It has no legislative power over member churches, but strong moral authority. There is a Sub-Unit for Dialogue with People of Living Faiths, which subsumes The Consultation on The Church and the Jewish People (CCJP). This itself is a successor to the International Missionary Council's Committee on the Christian Approach to the Jews (IMCCAJ), which was formed in 1931. CCJP is elected by the working group of the Sub-Unit and is composed of Christians who are concerned for the Jewish people and for the theological integrity of the church. Whereas IMCCAJ was almost exclusively oriented towards mission, CCJP is predominantly concerned for dialogue. In addition to its theological concern with the Jewish people, WCC, mainly through its Department on International Affairs, has made various comments on the situation in the Middle East.

1948–1982

At its first Assembly at Amsterdam in 1948, the WCC showed its awareness of Jewish suffering. 'We cannot forget that we meet in a land from which 110,000 Jews were taken to be murdered. Nor can we forget that we meet only five years after the extermination of 6 million Jews.'[1] Yet there was no hint of Christians being at least partly responsible for these sufferings. It was also made clear that the evangelistic task included the Jewish people. The church's failures in love and the 'image of the Jews as the sole enemies of Christ' (p. 70) which the church had often fostered were a hindrance to evangelism (not a cause of antisemitism!). Antisemitism was condemned clearly as a 'sin against God and Man'. The existence of Israel was noted, but the WCC did not express a judgment on the 'complex conflict of rights' (pp. 70f.).

At the Evanston Assembly (1954) an attempt was made to include a passage about the hope of Israel in the statement on 'Christ our Hope'. This was defeated, but those who moved it issued a statement explaining their convictions. They made clear that they hoped for the conversion of the Jewish people, but they also stressed the Jewishness of Jesus and God's concern for the Jewish people because of a wish to redress the 'grievous guilt of Christian people towards the Jews throughout the history of the Church'.[2]

At the 1961 New Delhi Assembly, the WCC repeated its condemnation of antisemitism and made clear that blame for the crucifixion should not fall upon the Jewish people of today. 'In Christian teaching the historic events which led to the Crucifixion should not be so presented as to fasten upon the Jewish people of today responsibilities which belong to our corporate humanity and not to one race or community' (p. 12).

In the following years the WCC's Faith and Order Commission and the CCJP pursued joint studies and a meeting in Bristol in 1967 agreed a report which in 1968, at Geneva, was commended for further study. The *Bristol Report*, as it is usually known, affirmed that in Jesus Christ, God's revelation in the Old Testament finds its fulfilment, and in him, God's covenant is opened to all people. It is manifest, however, that God has not abandoned the Jewish people, who do not believe in Jesus, and the hope was affirmed 'that his promise and calling will ultimately prevail so as to bring them to their salvation' (pp. 20f.). There was a split between those who said that the church alone was theologically the continuation of Israel and those who said that the Jews were still God's elect people, which implied that the 'one people of God is broken asunder' (p. 21).

These differences were reflected in different approaches to mission. 'If the main emphasis is put on the concept of the Church as the body of Christ, the Jewish people are seen as being outside. The Christian attitude to them is considered to be in principle the same as to men of other faiths and the mission of the Church is to bring them, either individually or corporately, to the acceptance of Christ, so that they become members of the body . . . If, on the other hand, the Church is primarily seen as the people of God, it is possible to regard the Church and the Jewish people together as forming the one people of God, separated from one another for the time being, yet with the promise that they will ultimately become one. (This approach) should be thought of more in terms of ecumenical engagement in order to heal the breach than of missionary witness in which she hopes for conversion' (pp. 23f.).

The Bristol document pointed to the need for further study of the authority of the Bible. It repeats rejection of the view that Jews were guilty of the death of Jesus. It warns against depicting Jews in a way that encourages antisemitism. It calls upon the churches to re-examine their liturgies and makes the important point that Judaism is more than the Old Testament.

At both the Uppsala (1968) and Nairobi (1975) Assemblies, statements were adopted about the Middle East situation, but there has been no discussion about the theological significance of Judaism and the Jewish people at a WCC Assembly since 1961.

At the Chiang Mai (Thailand) Consultation in 1977, the unique relationship of Jews and Christians was recognized, as was the need for Christians to eradicate antisemitism. The question of whether Jews and Christians have a mission and concerns in common was raised.

In the same year, a British Working Group of CCJP agreed a third revised text. Here, for the first time, the theological significance of 'the Land' is taken seriously. 'Judaism believes that there is a positive spiritual purpose in fulfilling as many of God's commandments as possible; the opportunity for this is at its highest in the Holy Land, where the commandments concerning the Holy Land and its produce may be observed, and where the sanctity to Judaism of worship in previous times is keenly felt. Thus the yearning of the Jewish People to be able to practise their religion in their land is, for them, a yearning of the highest degree of holiness and spirituality. In modern times, many Jews have therefore seen a strong, religious purpose in the strengthening of Jewish settlement in Israel.'[3]

The group also recognized that whereas Christianity has often defined itself over against Judaism, the Jewish revelation does not need Christianity at all for its self-definition. The need to listen to

Jewish self-understanding is stressed. The continuing election of the Jewish people is affirmed. 'Is it too much to hope that the people of the two covenants, the Church and Jewry – *together the continuing People of God* – may still stand in creative tension, enriching and encouraging each other, despite the appalling record of the relationship between the two communities over the centuries?' (pp. 162f.). The need to purge liturgies of anti-Judaism is again emphasized.

In the same year, 1977, the CCJP, meeting in Jerusalem, rejected proselytism as violating the rights of the human person, whilst affirming the call to witness to God's love for and claim upon the whole of humankind. Again there is disagreement about witness. 'Some of us believe that we have to bear witness also to the Jews; some among us are convinced, however, that Jews are faithful and obedient to God even though they do not accept Jesus Christ as Lord and Saviour' (p. 166).

Ecumenical Considerations

By 1982, after a long process of discussion to which some of the reports mentioned above contributed, the Executive Committee of the WCC 'received and commended to the churches for study and action' the document *Ecumenical Considerations on Jewish–Christian Dialogue*. This recognized the asymmetry of Jewish–Christian relations. It pointed to the need for Christians to unlearn their stereotyped images of Judaism and particularly to recognize that Judaism is a living religion, not 'a fossilized religion of legalism'.[4] 'Judaism in the time of Christ was in an early stage of its long life. Under the leadership of the Pharisees the Jewish people began a spiritual revival of remarkable power, which gave them the vitality capable of surviving the catastrophe of the loss of the temple. It gave birth to Rabbinic Judaism which produced the Mishnah and Talmud and built the structures for a strong and creative life through the centuries' (p. 38). Jesus, as a Jew, was born into this tradition.

Ecumenical Considerations recognized that the Jews never forgot the Land of Israel. 'There was no time in which the memory of the Land of Israel and of Zion, the city of Jerusalem, was not central in the worship and hope of the Jewish people. "Next year in Jerusalem" was always part of Jewish worship in the diaspora. And the continued presence of Jews in the Land and in Jerusalem was always more than just one place of residence among all the others' (p. 40).

Christian responsibility for Jewish sufferings was acknowledged. 'Teachings of contempt for Jews and Judaism in certain Christian traditions proved a spawning ground for the evil of the Nazi Holocaust' (p. 40). Proselytism was again rejected, but the disagreement about mission continued. 'There is a wide spectrum, from those who see the very presence of the Church in the world as the witness called for, to those who see mission as the explicit and organized proclamation of the gospel to all who have not accepted Jesus as their Saviour. This spectrum as to mission in general is represented in the different views of what is authentic mission to Jews. Here some of the specifics are as follows: There are Christians who view a mission to the Jews as having a very special salvific significance, and those who believe the conversion of the Jews to be the eschatological event that will climax the history of the world. There are those who would place no special emphasis on a mission to the Jews, but would include them in the one mission to all those who have not accepted Christ as their Saviour. There are those who believe that a mission to the Jews is not part of an authentic witness, since the Jewish people finds its fulfilment in faithfulness to God's covenant of old' (pp. 41f.).

Sigtuna 1988

The various statements by the WCC have recently been subject to review. Together with a selection of statements by member churches they have been published in *The Theology of the Churches and the Jewish People*. At a recent meeting at Sigtuna, Sweden, members of the WCC Consultation on the Churches and the Jewish People reviewed these documents to see what had been learned and to discern how far there was now a consensus in official church teaching.

In a statement issued after the CCJP Consultation at Sigtuna in November 1988, it is said that whilst WCC is committed to breaking down barriers and promoting the unity of the human family, the churches recognize that they have a special relationship with Judaism. It is widely agreed, the statement says, that:

1. The covenant of God with the Jewish people remains valid.
2. Antisemitism and all forms of the teaching of contempt for Judaism, especially teaching about deicide, are to be repudiated.

3. The living tradition of Judaism is a gift of God.

4. Coercive proselytism directed towards Jews is incompatible with Christian faith.

5. Jews and Christians bear a common responsibility as witnesses to God's righteousness and peace in the world.

The document recognizes that there is not yet a common mind in the churches on the question of mission nor on the relation of covenant and land, especially in relationship to the state of Israel.

CCJP, whose members represent a wide spectrum of Continental and North Atlantic Churches, agreed nine affirmations, which recognized Israel's call, acknowledged the spiritual treasures Christians share with the Jewish people, made clear that Jews must not be blamed for the passion of Jesus and expressed sorrow at the Christian share of responsibility for the sufferings of the Jews, which culminated in the Shoah.

Jesus' own solidarity with the Jewish people is stressed. 'Jesus in his ministry addressed himself primarily to Jews, affirmed the divine authority of the Scriptures and the worship of the Jewish people . . . He came to fulfil, not to abrogate the Jewish life of faith based on the Torah and the Prophets.' 'Yet,' the statement continues, 'by his proclamation of the dawn of the eschatological kingdom . . . messianic claims and above all his death and resurrection, Jesus inaugurated a renewal of the covenant.'[5] This was in time to lead to a new religious movement, but it is made clear that the split occurred after the time of Jesus, because of disagreements about the position of Gentiles and the demands of Torah. 'Two communities of faith gradually emerged sharing the same spiritual roots, yet making very different claims. Increasingly, their relations were embittered by mutual hostility and polemics' (p. 10).

It is affirmed that the Jews have not been rejected by God and that his promises continue. 'We see not one covenant displacing another, but two communities of faith, each called into existence by God, each holding its respective gifts from God, and each accountable to God' (p. 10).

The statement ends by affirming 'that the Jewish people today is in continuation with biblical Israel and we are thankful for the vitality of Jewish faith and thought. We see Jews and Christians, together with all people of living faiths, as God's partners working in mutual respect and co-operation for justice, peace, reconciliation and the integrity of creation' (p. 10).

The omission of affirmations on the Land or State of Israel and on Mission was bound to disappoint Jews. They felt that the World Council of Churches, which had often issued statements, hostile to Israel, on the political situation, was not committed to Israel's right to exist. They could still not be sure that conversionist activity had been abandoned in favour of dialogue.

2. Church statements

Besides the documents produced by the WCC, many statements have been produced by Protestant churches in Europe or North America. There are as yet none from the Orthodox churches nor from non-Catholic churches in Latin America, Africa or Asia.

Of particular interest are the 1985 reports by the Church of Scotland, the *Guidelines for Christian–Jewish Relations* from the American Episcopal Church (1987) and the document on *The Way of Dialogue* agreed at the 1988 Lambeth Conference of Anglican bishops. We shall consider them in reverse order.

The Lambeth Conference 1988

The Lambeth Conference of Anglican Bishops in 1988 commended the document *Jews, Christians and Muslims: The Way of Dialogue*. It is very unusual for the Lambeth Conference to commend a whole document, rather than a short resolution. That they did so, without a single vote against and without any abstentions, gives real weight to the document. It was the first time that the Anglican Communion had addressed the subject. The original draft referred only to Jews, but it was thought expedient to speak also of dialogue with Muslims.

The document begins with a sensitive description of dialogue, as 'the work of patient love and an expression of the ministry of reconciliation. It involves understanding, affirmation and sharing. The essential condition of any true dialogue is a willingness to listen to the partner; to try to see with their eyes and feel with their heart. For understanding is more than intellectual apprehension. It involves the imagination and results in a sensitivity to the fears and hopes of others. Understanding another means allowing them to define themselves in their terms rather than ours, and certainly not in terms of our inherited stereotypes.'[6] Later the document returns

to this subject, saying, 'Dialogue does not require people to
relinquish or alter their beliefs before entering into it; on the
contrary, genuine dialogue demands that each partner brings to it the
fullness of themselves and the tradition in which they stand. As they
grow in mutual understanding they will be able to share more and
more of what they bring with the other. Inevitably, both partners to
the dialogue will be affected and changed by this process, for it is
mutual sharing' (p. 305).

There are three parts to the document: 'The Way of Understanding', 'The Way of Affirmation' and 'The Way of Sharing'. Under 'The
Way of Understanding', it is affirmed that Judaism is a living religion
and that its definitive works, such as the Mishnah and the Talmud,
were produced by post-Pharisee rabbis – thus implicitly rejecting the
widespread misapprehension that Judaism is the religion of the Old
Testament. It is recognized that Judaism is not only a religion, but 'a
people and a civilization' (p. 299). 'It is against this background, at
once secular and religious,' continues the report, 'that the importance of the land of Israel to the majority of Jews throughout the world
needs to be understood' (p. 300). This is now the only reference to
the land or state of Israel, whereas the draft had a full section on this.
The Conference, in a different context, passed a resolution which
affirmed Israel's right to recognized and secure borders, but which
also affirmed 'the right of the Palestinians to self-determination,
including choice of their own representatives and the establishment
of their own state' (Resolution 24, p. 220).

Under the 'Way of Understanding', the 'profound changes and
potential for good' in modern scholarly understanding of the Bible is
recognized. This is increasingly a joint Jewish–Christian enterprise.
Such study shows Judaism in a more positive light and reveals the
political factors in the division between church and synagogue. 'Since
many of the factors in this split were contingent on specific historical
developments, and events need not necessarily have turned out the
way they did, there would seem to be no reason why a new
understanding should not develop, based on a reconsideration of
what originally drove Christianity and Judaism apart' (p. 300). This
seems to support the view that the real 'parting of the ways' occurred
after the fall of Jerusalem in CE 70. This implies that the Gospels
themselves are coloured by the polemic of that period and do not
accurately reflect Jesus' relationship to the faith and practice of his
people.

Under 'The Way of Affirmation', the special bond between Judaism and Christianity is recognized. It is suggested that the relationship would be strengthened if both traditions gave a central place to their hope for God's kingdom. Christians, it is said, naturally focus on Jesus the Christ and his church, but both realities 'can and should be seen within the hope for, and the horizon of, the Kingdom of God' (p. 302). It is also noted that 'Christians and Jews share a passionate belief in a God of loving kindness who has called us into relationship with himself' (p. 302) – a sentence which implicitly rejects the false contrast sometimes made between 'the God of the Old Testament' and 'the God of the New Testament'. The abiding covenant with Israel is recognized. There is also clear acknowledgment of Christian guilt for anti-Jewish propaganda, which has contributed so much to Jewish sufferings. The document confesses that anti-Jewish prejudice in the church has caused untold suffering and provided the soil in which 'the evil weed of Nazism was able to take root and spread its poison' (p. 303).

'The Way of Sharing' includes the section which was most hotly debated – namely about attempts to convert Jews. The document as it stands recognizes the variety of views within Christianity today. 'At one pole, there are those Christians whose prayer is that Jews, without giving up their Jewishness, will find their fulfilment in Jesus the Messiah. Indeed some regard it as their particular vocation and responsibility to share their faith with Jews . . . Other Christians, however, believe that in fulfilling the law and prophets, Jesus validated the Jewish relationship with God, while opening up this way for Gentiles through his own person. For others, the holocaust has changed their perception, so that until Christian lives bear a truer witness, they feel a divine obligation to affirm the Jews in their worship and sense of the God and Father of Jesus' (p. 305). This was probably as much as could have been accepted by the Conference, but it lacks the forward looking breadth of the draft. This suggested that Christian concern for Jews today should firmly reject any form of proselytizing which attempts to convert the individual Jew to Christianity. The relationship should express itself in *praise* for Jewish faithfulness, in *prayer* that they may be faithful to the Torah, in *service* which affirms and safeguards Jewish identity, in *listening* to the Jewish people and in *dialogue*, which includes mutual witness between equal partners.

Compared to the draft, the emphases on education, purging the liturgies, care in preaching, whilst still present, are diluted. The section on possible areas of common action is shortened. The historical section about Jews and Anglicans is omitted. This is a pity because it indicated that some Anglicans, such as James Parkes, were concerned for a new relationship early in the 1930s. Certainly Christian rethinking has been spurred on by the horrors of the Holocaust, but the historical perspective is a reminder that the primary basis for a new relationship is the question of truth and the proper understanding of the evidence.

The Church of Scotland

The Church of Scotland report on *Antisemitism in the World Today* (1985) also makes the point that the Church of Scotland's sensitivity to antisemitism is on record before knowledge of the extent of the Nazi outrage shamed all Christians. In 1934, the General Assembly of the Church of Scotland declared: 'Remembering the age-long sufferings of the Jewish people, their homelessness as a nation which has lasted for centuries, the persecutions, injustices and hardships they have endured, from governments, churches and from individuals; in view also of the present fresh outbreaks of antisemitic fanaticism manifested in many lands, the General Assembly offer to the Jewish people their heart-felt sympathy with them in their almost intolerable wrongs. The General Assembly of the Church of Scotland desire to assure the entire Jewish world that ill-treatment of Jews on account of their race or religion is to them abhorrent; that in their judgment it is a denial of the first principles laid down by the great Founder of the Christian Faith, who places love and kindness to all as fundamental laws of His Kingdom; and that it is their firm belief that any Church which claims to be animated by the spirit of Jesus Christ and which nevertheless acts with intolerance towards members of the Jewish race, is thereby denying the elementary doctrines of the Christian faith.'[7]

In its report *Christians and Jews Today* (1985), the Church of Scotland affirmed dialogue and the everlasting covenant of God with the Jewish people. It has particularly important sections on the Holocaust and on Israel. 'For Christians,' it says, 'the Holocaust requires a radical self-searching. It poses a dreadful question mark over the whole moral and spiritual basis of our Western European society.'[8] The report recognizes both that the Nazis were fundamentally opposed to the Gospel and that there was complicity by the churches. Grateful for 'righteous Gentiles', it is nonetheless affirmed that 'the fact remains that the Holocaust could never have taken place had the ground for it not been prepared by centuries of anti-Jewish polemic and persecution within Christendom . . . Without a confession of guilt, there can be no true dialogue' (pp. 55f.).

The report has a balanced and thorough discussion of the different views on 'mission', showing an awareness of how people put a variety of meanings on the same word. The report is also one of the very few to grapple with the theological significance of the creation of the state of Israel. The importance of Israel to almost all Jews is acknowledged and Jewish aspirations are sensitively presented. The report goes on: 'In the context of our belief that the Jewish people's election remains valid and the promises are theirs, we rejoice that they have returned to the Land and affirm their right to live there in peace and security. Such rejoicing is tempered by sorrow at the suffering of the Palestinians who also have the right to self-determination and human dignity' (p. 56). In the group some held that the creation of a homeland did not theologically necessitate a Jewish sovereign state. Others argued that 'since in the Hebrew Scriptures Israel was called to be both the People of God and a Holy Nation representative of all peoples and nations, it belongs to the purpose of God that Israel should still today be both a People and a Nation' (p. 57) – although it should still answer the stringent call of the prophets for righteousness. The group saw the dangers of over-simplistic application of biblical prophecy to contemporary events. The argument was mainly as to whether the promises relating to a literal return to the Land have been fulfilled in Christ and thus superseded in the same way as circumcision and the ceremonial law or whether the promises to the Land, like the moral Law, were not abrogated but confirmed in Christ. In the report on antisemitism, it is observed that anti-Zionism is often a covert form of antisemitism.

The American Episcopal Church

The American Episcopal Church's *Guidelines* (1987) also endorse dialogue and the need for a new understanding of Jews and Judaism. An interesting paragraph speaks of Jesus the Jew. 'Jesus was a Jew, born into the Jewish tradition. He was nurtured by the

Hebrew scriptures which he accepted as authoritative and interpreted both in terms of the Judaism of his time and in fresh and powerful ways in his life and teaching, announcing that the Kingdom of God was at hand. In their experience of his resurrection, his followers confessed him as both Lord and Messiah.'[9] Here there seems to be an awareness of the views of many biblical scholars that Jesus himself may not have claimed to be Messiah. A practical recommendation is that the relationship between Christians and Jews be observed liturgically each year, perhaps near Yom HaShoah or the Feast of St James of Jerusalem.

3. The unanswered theological challenge

The documents of the World Council of Churches and of member churches show that many of the misconceptions about Judaism have been repudiated, but there has been little reformulation of Christians' own beliefs. In a telling comment on the Lambeth 'Way of Dialogue', John Sargant, who helped to prepare a document on Anglican thinking about dialogue prior to the Lambeth Conference, says: 'It does not have the character of guidelines. What it seems to do best is to help Christians towards a more informed understanding of Judaism and Islam.'[10] This is desirable, but suggests that the theological challenges which would have to be faced before guidelines could be agreed have been evaded. The same comment still seems to be true of most statements agreed by members of the World Council of Churches.

3

Is there a Consensus in the Churches?

Agreement

There are several areas where there is general agreement in the churches on the Christian approach to Judaism.

First, the teaching of contempt is rejected. It is made abundantly clear that the Jews should not be charged with deicide. This charge is rejected on historical, theological and moral grounds. Historically, Jesus was crucified on orders of the Roman governor and he had Jewish supporters as well as Jewish opponents. Theologically, Jesus bears the sins of all humankind. Morally, it is wrong to blame successive generations for what their parents may have done. The need to purge the liturgy of 'contempt' is recognized. There is more uncertainty about how to treat those passages of the New Testament that seem anti-Jewish. Some suggest they should not be read in public, whereas others suggest the need for careful teaching and an introductory explanation before reading such passages. Gradually a fairer picture of the Pharisees is being accepted and it is being recognized that Judaism cannot be dismissed as 'legalism'. Judaism is acknowledged to be a living religion and the Rabbinic contribution is being recognized. Talk of the Second Temple period as 'late Judaism' is disappearing and Christians are less likely to think of Judaism as just 'Old Testament religion'. Jesus' Jewishness is affirmed, although there is still a tendency to exalt him by unfair comparisons with Judaism.

Secondly, the special bond linking Christians and Jews is recognized and it is affirmed that God's covenant with Israel continues. 'We believe,' says the Rhineland Statement, 'in the permanent election of the Jewish people as the people of God and

realize that through Jesus Christ the church is taken into the
covenant of God with his people.'[1] 'Throughout the centuries the
word "new" has been used against the Jewish people in biblical
exegesis . . . "new" means no replacement of the "old". Hence we
deny that the people Israel has been rejected by God or that it has
been superseded by the church' (p. 208). The Netherlands Council
of Churches speaks of 'the central biblical thought of God's
unfailing faithfulness to the Jewish people' (p. 211).

Differences

On other matters there is uncertainty or disagreement. There is
some uncertainty in the documents about the relationship between
church and Israel. Has the one covenant been opened to Gentiles in
Jesus Christ? Are there two parallel covenants? Is God's activity to
be recognized in all communities of faith? In part it is seen that how
people think is determined by their images of the church. Is it the
body of Christ or the people of God?

Difference of opinion about the relationship of the two covenants
underlies differences about mission. If Judaism is a valid way to
God, what is the purpose of seeking converts? The Texas Conference of Churches calls for 'avoidance of any conversionary intent or
proselytism' (p. 187). Whilst acknowledging the universal nature of
the mission of Christian churches, the Texas statement says,
'because of our unique relationship to Jews and Judaism, we believe
that the posture of dialogue and shared mission is the one
appropriate to the singular relationship' (p. 188). The Union of
Evangelical Churches in Switzerland, however, affirm that 'the
Christian witness cannot be exhausted by dialogue alone nor by
proclamation of the Word. It is credible only if every one, including
the Jews, is convinced through deeds' (p. 203).

There is little discussion of the place of Jewish Christians and
Messianic communities, nor perhaps recognition that continuing
mission impedes dialogue. To some Jews, Christian mission appears to seek the spiritual destruction of Judaism, which even Hitler
failed to achieve.

The Holocaust

Recent statements have begun to speak of the Holocaust and to
acknowledge Christian responsibility. The note of penitence is still
limited and reflection on the Holocaust has not, at an official level,

yet had much influence on Christian theology, in, for example, the understanding of God's power and love. The American Lutheran Church says: 'No Christian can exempt himself from involvement in the guilt of Christendom. But Lutherans bear a special responsibility for this tragic history of persecution because the Nazi movement found a climate of hatred already in existence. The kindness of Scandinavian Lutherans towards Jews cannot alter the ugly facts of forced labour and concentration camps in Hitler's Germany. That the Nazi period fostered a revival of Luther's own mediaeval hostility toward Jews, as expressed in pugnacious writings, is a special cause of regret. Those who study and admire Luther should acknowledge unequivocally that his anti-Jewish writings are beyond any defense' (p. 180).

The Lambeth document says that 'the systematic extermination of six million Jews and the wiping out of a whole culture must bring about in Christianity a profound and painful re-examination of its relationship with Judaism'.[2]

The Archbishop of Canterbury, Dr Robert Runcie, in his 1988 Kristallnacht Memorial address, went further: 'The travesty of Kristallnacht and all that followed is that so much was perpetrated in Christ's name. To glorify the Third Reich, the Christian faith was betrayed. The slaughter of the Jews was a desecration of the ministry of Jesus, himself a Jew. Neither inside nor outside Germany did the churches recognize this. And even today there are many Christians who fail to see it as self-evident. And why this blindness? Because for centuries Christians have held Jews collectively responsible for the death of Jesus. On Good Friday Jews have, in times past, cowered behind locked doors for fear of a Christian mob seeking "revenge" for deicide. Without the poisoning of Christian minds through centuries, the holocaust is unthinkable.'[3]

There is no struggling with the implicit anti-Judaism of traditional Christian affirmations about Jesus – what Rosemary Ruether called 'the left-hand of christology'. To say Jesus is Messiah can be heard as a negative comment on the Jewish people, most of whom failed to recognize him. Did he claim to be Messiah? He did not fulfil Jewish expectations. The world is not redeemed. Further, the titles applied to Jesus by the first believers, who were Jews, acquire a new significance when taken over by the Gentile Church. However, such issues that call for a profound rethinking of the Christian faith are not yet addressed in church statements.

The state of Israel

The statements show a little recognition of Israel's place in Jewish self-understanding. There is a wide variety of Christian theological views, perhaps most clearly outlined in the Church of Scotland report or the *Reflections* of the Union of Evangelical Churches in Switzerland[4] – but the tendency is to treat the issue as a political matter, identifying the Palestinians as 'the poor' of liberation theology. The Council of Churches in the Netherlands are particularly sympathetic to Israel's difficulties.[5]

There are many other issues which are not even touched upon, such as mixed marriages or the possibility of praying together, apart from one reference in a Vatican document. There is growing stress on the common responsibility of Jews and Christians together to uphold moral values and to serve the world. This was especially noticeable at the Second Official Anglican–Jewish consultation (1987).

The theological task is still waiting

The WCC Bristol Report (1967) said that 'there is no doctrine of Christian theology which is not touched and influenced in some way by this confrontation with the Jewish people'.[6] The Catholic Bishops of the USA have also spoken of a 'task incumbent on theologians, as yet hardly begun, to explore the continuing relationship of the Jewish people with God and their spiritual bonds with the New Covenant and the fulfillment of God's plan for both Church and Synagogue'.[7] But there has been little evidence of this. As the American theologian Paul van Buren points out, in none of the documents is 'there serious consideration of the implications of the church's growing awareness of the Jewishness of Jesus for the church's central christological doctrine'.[8] Further, as Allan Brockway of the World Council of Churches says, 'the churches – and for that matter, most theologians – have scarcely begun to examine some extremely difficult questions arising from their "rediscovery" of God's faithfulness to the ancient covenant', which ought to lead to the repudiation of all proselytism' (p. 186). The absence of any analysis of the relationship between the Jewish people and the land in all major WCC documents is also regrettable.

Allan Brockway ends his survey of WCC documents with these words: 'Those churches which incorporate the continuing reality of the covenant between the Jewish people and God into their official theology establish a premise with far-reaching implications, both for their relations with the Jewish people and for Christian theology itself. By and large, however, the development and implementation of those implications remain in the future' (p. 186). The churches have in large measure relearned their picture of Judaism. They have yet to grasp the theological implications of this for their own self-understanding.

I often suspect that more Jews read church statements on Christian–Jewish relations than do members of those churches which produce them. Certainly they are given more attention in the Jewish than the Christian press. Even so, the statements serve as a touchstone. They show that the churches have distanced themselves from traditional anti-Jewish teaching. The churches are also beginning to grapple with the Christian share of responsibility for the Holocaust and recognizing the importance of Israel to Jewish self-understanding. At last, the deeply entrenched missionary obligation is being questioned. Yet a proper appreciation of Judaism cannot leave our understanding of Christianity unaffected. It is this theological task that church synods hesitate to tackle lest they appear to be altering the 'faith once delivered to the saints'.

I recall that at the Arnoldshain meeting of CCJP in 1986 our group was meant to be discussing the impact of our new understanding of Judaism on our christology. About every five minutes the Orthodox member of the group reminded us that christology had been defined at the Council of Chalcedon in 451 so there was nothing to discuss. A similar assumption that nothing has really changed is seen in much of the talk about the 'Decade of Evangelism', starting in 1991, which appears oblivious to the fact of inter-faith dialogue.

Those who have devoted time and study to Christian–Jewish relations, including staff members who have worked on the statements discussed above, are aware of the far-reaching changes that the churches need to consider. In the second part of this book, I seek to share how my Christian faith has been reshaped through exposure to Judaism. I hope these personal reflections will encourage others to share this exciting exploration and may help Christians learn to affirm their faith without, albeit often unconsciously, at the very same time denigrating the faith of others.

PART TWO

Explorations

4

The Jewish Jesus

The first way in which knowledge of Judaism has altered my understanding of Christianity has been in clarifying my picture of Jesus. To recognize that Jesus was a faithful Jew is to understand Christianity in a new light. Indeed the increased emphasis on the Jewishness of Jesus has been called a 'minor revolution in biblical studies' with 'more far-reaching consequences than is generally realized'.[1]

It is not, of course, that Christians have been unaware that Jesus was Jewish.[2] The great reformer Martin Luther, who wrote with such vitriol against the Jews, wrote a tract in 1523, called *That Jesus Christ Was Born a Jew*. But Jesus has been set in opposition to Judaism, and it is still surprising to many Christians not only that Jesus was born a Jew, but that he died a Jew and not a Christian. For centuries Jews were reviled because they rejected Jesus.[3] Whilst such teaching has been repudiated, it is still common for Jesus to be exalted at the expense of Judaism. As one rabbi put it, radio talks often set him up over against the Pharisees and Jesus always wins 'six-love, six-love'.

It is necessary, then, to repudiate centuries of false teaching, to seek an accurate picture of first-century Judaism and to consider Jesus' relationship to it.

1. The changing picture of Jesus

The difficulties of speaking about the historical Jesus are well known, and any picture of him is liable to be more of a portrait of the author. Yet as a teenager, it was my picture of Jesus that attracted me to Christianity. I am aware how over the years that picture has been modified, although I am not over-confident that after reading so many books about Jesus, my present picture of him is even yet likely to be historically accurate. Indeed those who first introduced me to New Testament studies at Cambridge made very clear the complexity of reconstructing the historical ministry of Jesus. When I first started grappling with these problems, the German New Testament scholars Günther Bornkamm and Ernst Fuchs were just starting a renewed quest for the historical Jesus.[4]

Suddenly to find myself in a Hindu milieu was to look at the preoccupation with the historical from a new perspective. For Swami Vivekananda, one of the influential figures in the Hindu renaissance, the power of the gospel was independent of its actuality. 'It does not matter at all whether the New Testament was written within five hundred years of his birth, nor does it matter even how much of it is true . . . But there must have been a nucleus, a tremendous power that came down, a marvellous manifestation of spiritual power.'[5] Mahatma Gandhi, too, did not care whether the crucifixion was historically true or not. To him, he said, it was truer than history. Jesus was a teacher and exemplar of sacrificial love. His was the eternal message of the great teachers of humankind. This helped me to see that the power of the gospel story was not determined by its historical accuracy. The pursuit of the historical study of Jesus, although it might modify one's picture of him, was no longer a threat to faith. I realized that my faith-relationship to him was more a personal discipleship and a commitment to him and the values he embodied – above all in his self-giving love on the cross – than a judgment on historical evidence. To believe that God raised Jesus from the dead is, for me, an affirmation that sacrificial love is stronger than evil or death.

I realized, too, that there is no one right picture of Jesus. Just as in a family we each have our own relationship with and picture of the other members of it, so everyone makes his or her own response to Jesus. Indeed it is clear that in the New Testament itself the various authors painted different pictures of him. It is now recognized, too, that there are many theologies in the New Testament and that the attempt to write a 'New Testament theology' is misleading. Much argument in the church, therefore, seems pointless. Yet just as some people have a more intimate knowledge of others, so some people have a closer relationship with Jesus. The picture of him of those who first believed in him has continuing authority. We need to understand their message in its historical context to ensure our continuity in faith with them. We have also to recognize the role of the community of faith. Jesus Christ today is what he has become in two thousand years of devotion in the church. Historical study may be a corrective, but those who set a historical picture of Jesus over against the church's pictures of him need also to examine their presuppositions.

If Cambridge made me sceptical about the historical value of the Gospels and India made me think that this did not matter overmuch, study in Israel, at the Ecumenical Institute for Theological Research at Tantur, made the historical context of Jesus' ministry more vivid. The Jewish writer Dr Pinchas Lapide gives five reasons why he as a Jew feels close to Jesus. These are the setting in life, which includes the geography and topography of Israel with its fauna and flora; the languages of Hebrew and Aramaic; the Hebrew Bible as sacred scripture; Oriental imagination and concern for Israel. Travelling the countryside, much more than visiting churches built on traditional sites, gave me a feeling for the real historicity of Jesus. The seminars led by Dr Schlom Ben Chorim, a Jewish scholar who had studied the life of Jesus, helped me begin to see Jesus as a faithful Jew.[6]

I see Jesus now as fully human, yet as completely obedient to the Father as any human can be. In his closeness to the Father, he mirrored in his teaching and actions the boundless love of God. Those who knew him most intimately became convinced that in him they were close to the presence of God. In his obedience to what he understood to be the Father's will and following the way of non-violent love, he was condemned to death. His disciples, however, were convinced that such self-giving love had not been defeated but was stronger than evil and death. In seeking to explain what he meant to them, the disciples used the imagery and titles with which they as Jews were familiar.

The newness in Jesus is therefore in continuity with, not in contrast to, Judaism. Recognizing this has meant unlearning the false picture of Judaism, and especially of the Pharisees, which I had assumed. I had not in fact, however, until meeting with Jews, been aware of how hostile traditional Christian teaching had been. I think this is true of a number of Christians today, and I have found it useful at meetings to enquire how many were brought up to regard the Jews as guilty of the death of Jesus. It is good that the number is lessening, but the Jewish world has not forgotten the centuries during which the vile teaching of deicide was proclaimed from Christian pulpits. Christians have, therefore to be reminded of it, because without real penitence for the past no new relationship with Jews is possible.

Deicide

Traditionally, the church claimed that Jesus was the Messiah foretold in the Old Testament. The Jews, it was said, not only failed to recognize him, but were held to be responsible for his death ('deicide'). Fateful words in Matthew's Gospel (27.26), 'His blood be on us and on our children', were quoted to support this view. In punishment, the Jews, who were often spoken of as 'children of the devil' (John 8.44), were, the church claimed, exiled by God from the land of promise.

Melito, Bishop of Sardis in the second century, seems to have been the first to make the charge of deicide. Attacking the Jewish people, he said in a sermon: 'You have slain your Lord in the midst of Jerusalem. Hear all you families of man, and see [the strange murder] that has been committed . . . He who hung the earth in its place is hanged, he who fixed the heavens is fixed upon the cross . . . the Master has been insulted, God has been murdered, the king of Israel has been slain by an Israelite hand.'[7] One finds a similar position being adopted centuries later, when for example, in 1942, the Archbishop Kametko of Nietra repeated this teaching as Jewish leaders pleaded with him to intervene against the deportation of Slovakian Jews. 'It is not just a matter of deportation,' the Archbishop said. 'You will not die there of hunger and disease. They will slaughter all of you there, old and young alike, women and children, at once – it is the punishment that you deserve for the death of our Lord and redeemer, Jesus Christ – you have only one solution. Come over to our religion and I will work to annul this decree.'[8] Even in 1948, members of the German Evangelical Church could say that the Holocaust was 'God's punishment for the Jews' rejection and crucifixion of Christ and that they had only themselves to blame'.[9] In fairness, however, it should be said that this teaching was never used by the churches to justify mass murder. Jews had a protected if abject position. The teaching was used to explain why the Jews were a reprobate people, rejected and punished by God. Yet the teaching was to hand when Hitler wanted to use it for his evil purposes – even though he was anti-Christian as well as anti-Jewish.[10]

Through the Christian centuries, the death of Jesus has been blamed on the Jews. Often Jews would lock themselves in their homes on Good Friday for fear of the Christians. It is clear that centuries of anti-Jewish teaching prepared the way for the Holocaust. It is now widely agreed that it is historically, morally and theologically wrong to hold the Jews guilty of the death of Jesus. Historically, he suffered crucifixion, which was a Roman penalty. It is known that Pilate was a cruel ruler and anyone who was said to claim to be a king was likely to be in trouble. By the time the Gospels were written, Christians wanted to gain legitimacy in Roman eyes and seem to have shifted the blame for Jesus' death on to the Jews. Some Jews opposed him and the high priests, who may have felt their vested interest would be threatened by trouble with the Romans, may have been involved in a plot to be rid of him. The Pharisees were not involved. There is also considerable doubt about the nature and legality of 'the trial' of Jesus before the chief priests and the Council. Jesus had his supporters. There is no evidence, despite some hymns, that the Palm Sunday crowd which cried 'Hosanna' was the same as the mob which shouted 'Crucify'. Jesus seems to have been popular with the people. He was arrested at night to avoid a public outcry. Presumably, the secret that Judas betrayed was where Jesus could be secretly captured (Luke 22.4 and Mark 12.12). When he was crucified, other Jews mourned and lamented over him (Luke 23.27, 48). Those who became his first disciples were, of course, all Jewish.[11]

Morally it is wrong to hold a whole people guilty of the supposed wrong-doing of their ancestors. Young Germans today, for example, cannot be blamed for the evil deeds of the Nazis. Theologically, as the Vatican Council and other church synods have affirmed, God's covenant with his people has never been broken. Traditionally, also, the churches have taught that Christ died for the sins of all people.

Christian superiority

Although I was not brought up on this evil teaching of deicide, I read a book of sermons by the Anglican New Testament scholar Sir Edward Hoskyns called *We are the Pharisees*.[12] This depicted those involved in the trial and death of Jesus as embodying the evil of

which we all are capable. But the very title reflects the misunderstanding of Pharisaic Judaism which has been dominant. Indeed
unfavourable pictures of Judaism in the first century of the common
era (CE) have often been reinforced in historical and critical writing
on the New Testament. Although they are without the dogmatic
anti-Judaism of the past, they seek to affirm the significance of Jesus
by contrasting him with Judaism. There is a tendency to locate his
divinity at the point where he differs from the religion that nurtured
him. For example, W. Bousset, whose writings early in this century
have had considerable influence on subsequent German New
Testament scholars, admitted some formal similarities between
Jesus and his contemporaries, but denied any similarity on es-
sentials. 'In the one case we have mere exposition of the Scriptures,
in the other a living piety. There the parables are designed to
illustrate the distorted ideas of a dead learning . . . Here the
parable was handled by one whose soul was set . . . upon the
real.'[13]

A similar contrast is still to be found in 1989 in a book – in
intention sympathetic to Judaism – by Marvin R. Wilson of
Massachusetts. 'The love and compassion of Jesus knew no bounds,
his actions often proved radical or scandalous to the religious
community of his day.'[14] He quotes the British scholar John Riches'
summing up of Jesus' transformation of Judaism. Jesus 'sought a
renewal of the tradition by giving it a new direction: cutting away
attempts to multiply the detailed prescriptions of the Law and
directing them instead to personal standards as a means of
regulating conduct; rejecting the belief in God's punitive justice and
emphasizing instead God's mercy, his will to heal, to forgive, to
overcome enmity with love.'[15] Again, it has almost become a
commonplace of Christian scholarship to suggest that Jesus'
intimate sense of God as Father (abba = 'Daddy') is unique, but the
evidence does not seem to support this. The rabbis do in fact
address God as 'my Father', which is essentially the same.[16]

This approach, which exalts Jesus at the expense of Judaism,
belittles and distorts Judaism. A misleading contrast is made
between law and gospel, and the New Testament caricature of the
Pharisees is taken at face value. The revolutionary nature of seeing
that Jesus was a faithful Jew is to see him as one with the religious
leaders, not in opposition to them. As Fr John Pawlikowski, one of
the Catholic leaders of dialogue in America, writes: 'the basic link

between Jesus and Judaism must be sought in his sharing of the revolutionary vision of Pharisaic Judaism.'[17]

Pharisaic Judaism

There is much dispute about first-century Judaism because our main sources date from a later period. Rabbinic Judaism was codified from the second century CE. 'Many rabbinic debates reflect the new situation which existed after the destruction of Jerusalem and the temple in the year 70, when Judaism had to adapt to a totally new situation.' Even so, as Rabbi Michael Hilton and Fr Gordian Marshall go on to say in their joint study of *The Gospels and Rabbinic Judaism*: 'The oral transmission of rabbinic ideas was very important and the rabbinic texts clearly reflect much earlier material.'[18] We can have a general picture of Pharisaic Judaism, but detailed arguments about influence or primacy are likely to be unhelpful.[19] We also know, through the discovery of the Dead Sea Scrolls and other material, that Judaism in the first century CE was far more varied than is suggested by the Gospels or the Jewish historian Josephus.[20] This may be seen, for example, in the growing tendency to place the Fourth Gospel in a Jewish rather than a Hellenistic milieu.[21]

Covenant and Torah

If Christians are to understand the Jewish setting in which Jesus grew up, they need to rid themselves of false stereotyped pictures of Judaism. This means trying to understand the Judaism of the period for itself. Only then should the Gospel records be evaluated. They should not be taken as a reliable source for knowledge of Judaism in the first century CE.

Judaism should be understood in terms of the Covenant. God promised to Abraham that he would bless his descendants. God rescued the people of Israel from slavery in Egypt and chose them to be his own people. The Torah was given by God to those whom he had chosen by grace for his own. The Torah was the way of life for a community, and God gave Israel the land of promise where it could be a holy people. Circumcision was the sign of membership of the holy people.

To obey the Torah was to affirm the covenant and to accept God's promise. It was the loving response to God's gracious act of rescue and his choice of Israel to be his own, just as Christians, in

thankfulness for Jesus' love, seek to obey his will. Too often
Christians have pictured the law as a burden rather than as a delight.
The influence of Luther and the way Paul has often been interpreted
has been strong. This attitude is reflected in hymns like 'Rock of
ages' which has the lines,

> 'Not the labours of my hands
> Can fulfil thy law's demands,'[22]

or 'With a broken heart', with the words,

> 'Nor alms, nor deeds that I have done,
> Can for a single sin atone'.[23]

Here there is stress on the penitent's utter worthlessness and the
uselessness of all righteous works, which carries with it implicit
criticism of the supposed barren legalism and works-righteousness
of Judaism. In fact joyful obedience, springing from thankfulness
for God's mercy, is characteristic of Jewish devotion. A good
example is Psalm 119, where the Psalmist says, 'I love your
commandments more than gold, more than the finest gold' (v. 127),
or, 'Lord how I love your law, it is my meditation all the day long'
(v. 97).

Ed Sanders in his detailed studies of Jewish material in *Paul and
Palestinian Judaism* and *Jesus and Judaism* has shown in detail that
to regard Judaism as a religion of righteousness gained by
meticulous observance of the requirements of the law 'is based on a
massive perversion and misunderstanding of the material'.[24] God
chose Israel. Obedience to the Torah shows a reliance on God's
fidelity, not a concern to win his favour. The debates about
atonement show that there was a means by which the penitent
sinner could be restored to a right relationship to God, a relationship established by God's mercy and maintained by the
individual's obedience and repentance and by God's
forgiveness.[25]

The Pharisees

The origins of the Pharisaic movement are uncertain, but by the end
of the Maccabean period, in the first century BCE., they were
bringing about a far-reaching change in Judaism, which has had a
continuing influence up to the present day. The Pharisees had a new
perception of the relationship of God to human beings. God was not

just the God of the patriarchs nor just the parent of Israel, but the God of every individual. God watched over and cared for each person. New names were given to God, such as *Makom* ('The All-Present'), or *Ha-Kadosh Baruch Hu* ('The Holy One, Blessed Be He'), or *Abinu She-Bashamayim* ('Our Father who art in Heaven').[26]

As a direct result of the new understanding of the God–human relationship, the Pharisees taught belief in the resurrection – a teaching which brought them into conflict with the Sadducees, who were the high-priestly party. It was amongst the Pharisees that the position of rabbi, or teacher, emerged. They also developed the synagogue, as a place for communal assembly. Whilst not opposing the Temple ritual, they gave a symbolic interpretation to the sacrifices and insisted that they had no efficacy apart from genuine repentance and reparation.

The Pharisees' teaching about the covenant and Torah was true to the biblical teaching as already outlined. They called for obedience in response to God's mercy. Pharisaism, which was a lay movement, took seriously the obligation laid upon Israel as a whole to be a 'holy nation' before God. Purity was not just for priests at the Temple, but for all God's people. Taking the call to holiness seriously, the Pharisees sought to apply the law to contemporary life and here disagreed with the Sadducees, the high-priestly party, who stuck to a literal and often out-of-date interpretation.

The Torah was the major source of information on ordering the cult – the Temple worship – but it also showed the way of life that God expected. It was, however, seldom precise enough to show the exact behaviour required, whilst, of course, life changes, and laws have to be reapplied to new circumstances. There therefore grew up a cumulative reinterpretation and application of the Torah. Some of it was based on interpretation of a passage of scripture; some of it took the form of a pronouncement by a rabbi, and in addition there are stories which illustrate the teaching. In interpreting the Law, the Pharisees were guided by two principles. One was to build a fence around the Torah; the other was to make explicit what was implicit or unsaid.[27] John Bowker of Cambridge University, who has made a particular study of Rabbinic material, suggests that 'the people welcomed the assistance of the Hakamim (the learned) in alleviating the strictest interpretation of Torah and in defending their traditional ways'.[28]

The Pharisees also stressed table fellowship (*Haburah*).[29] To belong to a fellowship a person had to undertake certain obligations of purity and a disciplined way of life. The aim was to regard the whole world, not just the Temple, as the sanctuary where God dwells. Inevitably these rules separated the Pharisees from ordinary people, in the way Masons or vegetarians may separate themselves. There is no evidence, however, that they expected everyone to obey those self-chosen rules nor that they thought the common people were excluded from salvation.[30] The picture some Christians have of the Pharisees as an exclusive group looking down on others is not supported by the evidence. The sinners with whom Jesus mixed were not 'the common people', but quislings and criminals.

Jesus' arguments with the Pharisees, as reported in the Gospels, were no greater than the arguments amongst the Pharisees. Just as there were sharp differences amongst the Rabbis, for example between Hillel and Shammai, so it seems there were also sharp differences amongst the Pharisees. Yet, 'more important than the divisions were the far greater unities of methods, beliefs and intentions which they held in common, and which differentiated them as a whole from, for example, the Sadducees or the communities on the shores of the Dead Sea'.[31] There also seems to have been growing criticism of extremist elements, who appear to have been known as *perushim*, who stressed a very literal and detailed interpretation of Torah as the only way to holiness. The criticism of these extremists in rabbinic sources is similar to criticisms of them made in the Gospels.[32]

2. Jesus in a Jewish milieu

The Gospels reflect the concerns of the Christian community

Unravelling the evidence and seeing Jesus in a Jewish milieu is complex. Our knowledge of Jesus is mediated by the early Christian community. The Gospels reflect their concerns and indeed their polemic against Jews who did not believe in Jesus. It is generally agreed that the earliest Gospel, Mark, was written about thirty years after the death of Jesus. Luke and Matthew were perhaps written at least ten years later, although they used material from Mark. By the time they wrote, Jerusalem had fallen to the Romans (70 CE) and the acrimony between those Jews who did and those who did not believe in Jesus was intense.[33] The Jewish Christian

community had fled to Pella in Perea, before Jerusalem fell –
probably between 66–68 CE. Their 'desertion' alienated other
Jews. Further, by leaving Jerusalem, their ties with the Temple and
the rest of the Jewish community were weakened. About this time
believers in Jesus 'were put out of the synagogue'. This is reflected
in the Fourth Gospel, where the term 'Jews' is used of the
opponents of Jesus, even though some at least of the Johannine
community were Jewish believers in Jesus.[34] As a result all the
gospels reflect the bitter disputes that were taking place at the time
they were written, between members of the early church and many
Jews. They do not give an accurate picture of events during Jesus'
ministry. Even before the material in the Gospels was written
down, it had circulated orally in the Christian community for some
thirty years. During this time it had been shaped by its use in
worship, teaching and preaching. The sayings of Jesus cannot, with
any assurance, be taken to be his very words. Any reconstruction of
his life and ministry has to be pursued with great caution and
hesitancy.[35]

Further, the Christian community's faith and hope centred on the
belief that God had raised Jesus from the dead. This belief and the
conviction that Jesus was Lord were projected on to accounts of his
ministry. It is questionable, for example, whether Jesus predicted
that he would rise again. The disputes about his person and
authority in the Fourth Gospel highlight the theological issues, but
should not be taken as a report of actual arguments. Any
reconstruction of Jesus' life and ministry is bound to be very
tentative. The christological claims and the polemic against the
Pharisees are written into the Gospel account of Jesus' ministry,
after the event. Further, because any reconstruction of the historical Jesus is so tentative, it is unsafe to base claims for him by
contrasting him with his contemporaries.[36]

Jesus and the Pharisees

The criticism of the Pharisees in the Gospels should not disguise the
fact that Jesus was close to them in his teaching, in which he called
upon all Israel to acknowledge the rule of God. The pattern of his
ministry with its emphasis on teaching and reinterpretation of the
oral Torah and on healing of the sick is that of an authentic rabbi.
Like the Pharisees, he emphasized the *Shema* ('Hear, O
Israel . . .') and the importance of love. He taught the resurrection

of the dead. He stressed his intimate link with the Father. His meals
with his disciples, including the Last Supper, are similar to the
Pharisees' meals.[37]

It seems that Jesus did not observe the Pharisaic rules about
washing before meals, ritual purity and about table fellowship,
which may have surprised the Pharisees. Further, where there was
evident personal faith and repentance, even amongst sinners, Jesus
seems not to have been too concerned about the detailed requirements of the Law. Bowker suggests that amongst the Pharisees
'there were those who emphasized that the yoke of the Law was
easy and the burden light, . . . (to whom) the first imperative was to
encourage people to set themselves within the intention of keeping
the covenant; after that the details could be added as a constantly
extending act of love towards God'. For others, the whole Law was
meant to be kept and the details were as important as the general
spirit.[38] Jesus, Bowker suggests, made the extreme deduction from
the first view that 'the first and only step to be taken is in the
direction of God. Thus his *kelal*, or summary, of Torah is the love of
God and love of one's neighbour as oneself.'[39]

Whereas Jewish teaching saw repentance as a precondition for
forgiveness, Jesus appears to have offered sinners inclusion in the
kingdom while they were still sinners and before they had made the
customary offerings (Mark 1.40–2.12). He seems to have believed
that the initiative in seeking for the sinner was taken by God, who
sought for the lost sheep and welcomed the lost son. He also may
not have required of sinners repentance as normally understood.
His companions would therefore, at least technically, remain
sinners. 'It seems to be the case,' writes E. P. Sanders, 'that Jesus
offered the truly wicked – those beyond the pale and outside the
common religion by virtue of their implicit or explicit rejection of
the commandments of the God of Israel – admission to *his* group
(and, he claimed, the kingdom) *if* they accepted him.'[40]

Yet, despite possible differences of emphasis, E. P. Sanders
argues that 'We *know* of no substantial dispute about the Law, nor
of any substantial conflict with the Pharisees.'[41] Jesus did not reject
the Mosaic dispensation, but he no longer regarded it as final,
because a new age was dawning.[42]

Eschatological expectation, not disputes about the Law, seems to
have been the key point on which Jesus and his followers differed
from his contemporaries. He did not attack the covenant and

Torah, but his conviction that a new age was dawning gave him a new perspective on Judaism.

Eschatology

Jewish eschatological expectation in the first century CE was varied and far from clear-cut, just as Christian pictures about the Second Coming are imprecise. There was a general belief that this present age would give way to a new age of peace, righteousness and justice, when the faith of the righteous would be vindicated. The new age would be preceded by a period of deep distress, 'the Messianic Woes'. Some hoped for a universal salvation that would include the Gentiles and there was hope of a general resurrection. Jerusalem would remain central in the new age. There is not much literature about Messianic expectations, and this has probably been given greater emphasis by Christian scholars than it deserves. The Messiah would be a descendant of David, who would lead God's people. Some expected the end to be ushered in by a decisive act of God; others, such as the Zealots, expected a political revolution.

Although speculation about the end of the world was a significant part of Pharisaic teaching, it was the absorbing concern of the Essenes, the community who withdrew to the Dead Sea.[43] Whereas the Pharisees tried to be holy within society, the Essenes rejected society and were hostile to other Jews. They lived a strict ascetical life and saw themselves as Sons of Light struggling with the Sons of Darkness. It has been suggested that John the Baptist, and perhaps Jesus, had some contacts with the Essenes, but this remains speculative.

Jesus' preaching of the kingdom

Jesus seems to have been convinced that the new age was dawning with his ministry. Whereas the early church preached about Jesus, his own message was that 'The kingdom of God is at hand'. E. P. Sanders, in discussing the new age, focusses on the cleansing of the Temple, which, he argues, was a symbolic prophetic action. He rejects the view that Jesus was objecting to the dishonesty of the money-changers or to the trading as such, which was necessary for the sacrificial cult. Jesus was not just demonstrating against an abuse, but threatening the Temple itself, as is implied by the charges brought against him at his trial. The driving out of the animals signified the end of the sacrificial system. The over-turning of the tables foreshadowed the Temple's destruction. This, Sanders says, was in line with Jewish eschatological expectation. The coming of the 'new age' would mean 'a new temple'. In the Temple Scroll, God says, 'I shall sanctify my sanctuary with my glory: I shall cause my glory to dwell upon it until the Day of Blessing, when I myself shall create my sanctuary, establishing it for myself for ever, like the covenant which I made with Jacob at Beth-El.'[44]

Besides the expectation of a new Temple, there was also a hope that the twelve tribes of Israel would be restored. This gives significance to Jesus' choice of twelve disciples.[45] There is some disagreement about their names, but not about their number – and the number twelve had to be maintained after Judas' suicide. It was also expected that in the new age, the outcasts of Israel would be gathered in.[46] This would give added point to Jesus' emphasis on going to the sinners and outcasts. There was a further expectation that the in-gathering would include the Gentiles.[47] This was not to be part of Jesus' own ministry, but would explain why for Paul the conviction that Jesus was the Christ and his commission to preach to the Gentiles belonged together. In the new age, too, the Torah takes on a different significance.

Jesus, it seems, believed that with his ministry a new age was dawning. This points also to a self-consciousness and awareness of a special vocation[48]. His contemporaries recognized that he spoke with authority and that the cleansing of the Temple also raised the question of authority. This became the key issue. In words attributed to the disciples who journeyed to Emmaus on Easter Day, attention moves to Jesus himself: 'We hoped that He was the One who would deliver Israel.'[49]

Good people disagree

The new age was not a rejection of the past, nor a condemnation of Judaism, nor an abandonment of the covenant. Rather, it opened the mercy of God to all people. A number of people today speak about a 'new age' and there are many so-called 'new age groups'. Are we at the edge of a fresh stage in the development of human potential and spiritual consciousness? We do not know and good people can disagree. The tragedy is that the polemic that accompanied the disagreements in the first century has been carried forward through the ages. Gradually as we disentangle the theological from the political and sociological causes of 'The Parting of the Ways', we can recognize the sincerity and deep religious concern of both those Jews who believed in Jesus and those who remained faithful to the traditional understanding of Torah.[50]

To many Jews the world is not redeemed – the wars, the violence, the hunger, the torture, the homelessness, seem to confirm their view. With the coming of the Messiah, it is believed, all these evils will be done away. Jesus does not meet the Jewish expectation of the Messiah. The Christian believes that the inner change effected by Jesus will eventually result in world-wide change. Yet the Jewish 'no' is a warning to Christians not to spiritualize redemption and forget about the need to change the world. There is a warning also not to equate the church with the kingdom of God, but to remember that the church exists to make known God's love for the whole world. Paul van Buren speaks of the tremendous cover-up which had occurred before Christianity was even one hundred years old. 'What it had not accomplished, including such minor details as the end of human suffering, sickness, injustice, oppression and torture, death, much of it horrible . . . – all such details were simply scaled down in value in the mythological scenario as being of only transient concern. After all, with eternal life won, why care about actual human life? The more triumphalistic the mythological interpretation of Easter, the more Christianity could calmly ignore the world which it claimed that God so loved.'[51]

Seeing Jesus as a faithful son of the covenant requires us to affirm God's presence in him without a negative evaluation of Judaism. Indeed, we should point out how in what he says and does he is in harmony with his Jewish heritage. Christian congregations need to be helped to understand the general principles of New Testament criticism.[52]

The widespread assumption is still that the Gospels are in the main an accurate description of what Jesus said and did. In fact, they are an interpretation of his ministry written down some decades after the resurrection. Together with a programme of education and careful preaching, those who lead public worship should consider attentively the content of passages selected for public reading and of all material used in worship.[53]

Historical revision, however, is not enough. Traditional christological claims have also to be reconsidered. The church's Council of Chalcedon in 451 defined Jesus as being of two natures in one person. The Chalcedonian Definition, as this summary is known, speaks of him as very God and very man. We have to escape the shackles of Chalcedon as well as the distortions of the New Testament.

5

Questioning Christology

To see Jesus as a faithful Jew may help Christians to revise their distorted picture of Jewish faith and practice at the time of Jesus. Yet their faith that Jesus is Lord seems unavoidably to be a critique of Judaism. Indeed the radical American Catholic theologian Rosemary Ruether put the issue bluntly when she said that the left hand of christology was antisemitism. 'Is it possible,' she asks, 'to say "Jesus is Messiah" without, implicitly or explicitly, saying at the same time "and the Jews be damned"?'[1] To say, as Christians so often do, that Jesus was the Messiah or 'King of the Jews' carries with it the implication that the Jews did not recognize their Messiah when he came. Even if Jews are no longer blamed for this, the assumption is that they were or are spiritually blind and that their religion is inferior.

Rosemary Ruether's challenge has provoked much discussion in the USA, but very little in Britain. Is it possible to affirm faith in Jesus without a negative comment on Judaism? I believe it is and that it is vital to do so, if we are to overcome anti-Judaism. The German theologian Friedrich-Wilhelm Marquardt stresses that 'We will only have Christian anti-Judaism behind us when theologically we will have succeeded in making positive sense of the Jewish "no" to Jesus.'[2]

This is a complicated task and means questioning many widely-held assumptions. The first is that Jesus claimed to be or spoke of himself as God. It has already been suggested that his message was about the coming kingdom of God and not about himself. A careful study of the titles used of him – or apparently by him – in the Gospels suggests that these titles were given to him by the first believers in the early Christian community and were not ones that he himself claimed.

Secondly, those who first used these titles were Jews, schooled in strict monotheism. Whilst the conviction that God had raised Jesus from the dead – with the special relationship to the Father that this implied – was the formative belief of the early Christian community, the titles applied to him by the first Jewish believers acquired a rather different meaning when taken over by Gentile believers.

In the early church many titles were used of Jesus and various christologies are apparent. During the fourth and fifth centuries, by which time Christianity had become the official religion of the Empire, the belief of the church was more rigidly defined at the Councils of Nicaea, Constantinople and Chalcedon. What were deemed heretical views were now excluded.

From that period until this century, most Christians have assumed a fixed definition of the true faith. But this is to ignore the fact that the creeds themselves are historically conditioned. They did not drop from heaven, but are the product of majority votes at church councils, at which political influences were often strong. The language and thought forms are also historically conditioned. Words alter their meanings and metaphysical and philosophical presuppositions change. Someone, therefore, repeating the creed today may not mean exactly the same as those who first drafted it.

The emphasis on credal definition has, to my mind, a further serious difficulty. It gives the impression that faith is primarily intellectual, an agreement with propositions accepted as true. The biblical understanding of faith is of a relationship with the living God. The titles used of Jesus are therefore better understood as the language of worship and adoration than as metaphysical or ontological statements. By this I mean that when we call Jesus 'Lord' or 'Saviour', we affirm what he means for us. This is the language of discipleship and commitment. By turning it into a general statement we imply that 'Our Lord' must be the Lord for all people. To speak of him as Son is to affirm that in Jesus we are met by God himself. It should not be an attempt to define the being of the deity.

Seen in this way, Christian claims for Jesus need not be as threatening as they have often appeared to people of another faith. The claims belong to the language of affirmation and adoration – making plain the Christian belief that God has revealed himself in Jesus. They need not carry the negative implication that such revelation is only in Jesus, nor are they the departures from monotheism of which some Jews and Muslims accuse Christians.

To affirm faith in Jesus without a negative comment on the faith of others may free us to consider whether that other faith has something significant to say to us. My own view, as I shall argue later when we consider the relationship of world religions to each other, is that God's saving presence is known in all the great religions. As we listen to the difficulties that Jews and Muslims especially have with traditional Christian claims for Jesus, we may see that the way in which we have presented those claims may be misleading. In particular, the Easter faith has often been proclaimed in a triumphalist manner, which has seemed to ignore the continuing reality of evil.

1. The Titles of Jesus

There has been much debate about the titles used of Jesus, especially the title 'Son of Man'. In my view, Jesus did not use these titles himself and did not himself claim divinity. Those who first used most of the titles were Jews. They believed that God had come close to them in Jesus and that with the raising of Jesus from the dead, a new age had dawned. The titles they used were drawn from their Jewish heritage, which spoke of divine agents such as angels or personified divine attributes such as Wisdom or Logos.[3] As after the resurrection they read the scriptures, these Jewish followers of Jesus discovered a christological significance in many passages. Familiar titles were given a new meaning. Yet when these same titles were taken over by Gentile Christians, who were used to a different thought-world, the titles subtly changed their meaning and acquired a more metaphysical or ontological significance.

The titles of Jesus originated in the early church

Those who believed that God had raised Jesus from the dead believed that the New Age had indeed dawned. Increasingly, in the light of the resurrection, they focussed attention on Jesus himself rather than on his message of the kingdom. The Gospel material is shaped by this concern, so it is impossible to be sure how Jesus himself understood his role in the coming kingdom. Much critical study suggests that most of the titles used of Jesus in the Gospels derive from the early Christian community. It is widely accepted by critical scholars that the titles were not invented by Christians. They can be found in other contemporary documents. Probably it was the early Christians who adapted them to express their belief in Jesus, thereby giving them a new meaning. It is noticeable that each part of the New Testament has its own particular emphases and christo-logical picture.

Did Jesus claim a title for himself?

It seems unlikely that Jesus used of himself the titles Messiah, Son of God or even Son of Man. The German New Testament scholar Hanz Conzelmann has summarized his study of the titles used of Jesus in the New Testament like this. 'How then did Jesus regard himself? The answer cannot be given by a christological concept. It must come through a demonstration of how Jesus associated the announcement of the kingdom of God with himself as a sign. Of course christology is implied here. It will have to be developed after Easter.'[4] In a similar way, the Catholic scholar Raymond Brown writes: 'If Jesus presented Himself as one in whose life God was active, He did so not primarily by the use of titles, or by clear statements about what He was, but rather by the impact of His person and His life on those who followed Him.'[5]

Messiah

Because of Christian claims that Jesus was the long-awaited Messiah, overmuch attention has been paid to first-century Messianic expectation, giving it an exaggerated importance. It seems clear that the Messiah of Jewish expectation was not a divine figure, that Jesus did not fit Messianic expectations and that he did not claim to be Messiah. It is wrong, therefore, to accuse Jews of failing to recognize their Messiah.

Although Jewish expectation was varied, the Messiah was not thought of as a divine figure. 'By origin,' Conzelmann writes, 'the "Messiah" belongs to the nationalistic type of Jewish eschatology. "Anointed" is a designation of the king in the Old Testament. Thus from the beginning the Messiah is no supernatural figure, but a human saviour. Of course, over the course of time the different types of hope coalesce, and with them the idea of the saviour. The figure of the Messiah is accentuated until it becomes transcendent. But basically Messiahship always remains alien to apocalyptic thought . . . For a saviour only fits into the restoration of the earthly kingdom of Israel, and not into the kingdom of God which comes from above. So in Judaism, Messiah and kingdom of God are not conceptually linked, the idea that the Messiah brings in the kingdom of God is missing.'[6] The Messiah was expected to be, Conzelmann argues, an earthly deliverer, not a divine figure. This is probably true, but as I have pointed out, speculation about the coming of the Messiah was as varied and as imprecise as Christian thinking today about the Second Coming.

Jesus did not fit Jewish expectation. As Allan Brockway writes: 'The activity of Jesus bears little resemblance to the Jewish picture of the Messiah. The history of the Church does not bear out any claim that Jesus initiated the messianic age,' because an age of peace and justice has manifestly not come on earth. In the New Testament, 'Christ' becomes a name and links Jesus' death to the work of salvation. 'To equate the concepts,' Brockway continues, 'does violence to the Jewish hope for the Messiah; it hinders if it does not block the Church's proper development of cogent christologies.'[7]

Jesus was not the 'Messiah' whom Judaism expected and therefore the negative conclusion that the Jews rejected their Messiah is invalid. Even so, the church continues to sing the Advent hymn which has the verse:

> Every eye shall now behold him
> Robed in dreadful majesty;
> Those who set at naught and sold him,
> Pierced and nailed him to the tree,
>   Deeply wailing,
> Shall the true Messiah see.[8]

The Jewish and Christian uses of the term 'messiah' have come to bear about as much similarity to each other as the post-war use of 'democratic' by both East and West Germany in the titles of their countries.

It is in any case improbable that Jesus himself claimed to be Messiah. The title is used seven times in Mark's Gospel. It is used as a title in the opening verse of the book. It is used in the saying about a cup of water (9.41, but compare Matt. 10.42), in mockery (15.32), in the apocalyptic in chapter 13 (21) and in the dispute over Davidic sonship (12.35). The two most interesting occasions when the term is used are in Mark's account of Peter's confession (8.30) and of the high priest's question to Jesus during his trial at the high priest's house (14.62). Of the former, the New Testament scholar Dennis

Nineham, in a widely-read commentary on the Gospel of Mark, writes: 'The story is not so much intended to describe faithfully what happened on the *first* occasion when Jesus was recognized as Messiah as to show what is esssentially involved and demanded whenever such a recognition takes place.'[9] The latter verse raises very difficult questions about the historicity of the accounts of the trials of Jesus, which seem to defy almost all known Jewish rules of procedure. Again it seems that the theological content of the passage was what mattered to the evangelist, not the historicity.[10] It seems probable, therefore, that the use of Messiah in Mark's Gospel derives from the evangelist and not from Jesus himself. If Jesus did use the title of himself, he would have needed radically to reinterpret contemporary understanding of messiahship, perhaps, as is sometimes suggested, in the light of the Suffering Servant passages in Isaiah.

Certainly, quite early, Christians used the title Christ of Jesus, but it is a title that soon becomes a proper name. There is therefore considerable ambiguity about the claim that Jesus was Messiah. The Jewish 'no' to Christian claims that he was Messiah may be seen as faithfulness to their own understanding of Messiahship and as a necessary corrective to any tendency of Christians to spiritualize redemption.

Son of God and Lord

In a similar way, the Jewish use of the term 'Son of God' is radically different from its use by Gentile Christians. In the Old Testament, both Israel and the king are called 'son of God'. It was a term suggesting special favour and responsibility.

It is improbable that Jesus used the term of himself. The use of the title in Mark's Gospel seems clearly the work of the evangelist. It is used in the opening verse of the Gospel (1.1), used of Jesus at his baptism (1.11), used by those possessed with demons, who were thought to have supernatural insight (5.8), and used at the transfiguration (9.8). The title is used also at the trial by the high priest. On behalf of the Jews, he rejects its application to Jesus (14.62). By contrast, the Roman centurion, a Gentile, at the foot of the cross confesses: 'Truly this man was the (or a) Son of God' (15.39). If this use of the title is the evangelist's, then there is the possibility that his account of the baptism and transfiguration of Jesus are theological statements, not historical accounts. We do not, however, have theevidence to speculate about Jesus' self-consciousness or his own understanding of his mission or status.

To the first believers, who were Jewish, Jesus' sonship would have been understood in moral, not physical terms. It would have implied his total obedience to the Father's will. The Hellenistic world thought in terms of divine paternity, as is shown in the idea of his miraculous conception.[11] Gentile Christians, therefore, came to understand the title more literally than the first Jewish believers. We need to reverse the process, changing, as Pawlikowski suggests, 'our attitude toward the statement "Jesus is Son of God" and "Jesus is divine" from simple equation to interpretation'.[12]

The use of the title Kyrios, Lord, shows even more clearly the change from the primitive community to Hellenistic Christianity. Again by a comparison of the Gospels, it appears it was a term introduced by the evangelists, especially Luke. It was perhaps already in use within some of the early Christian communities. Yet its use by Jewish believers did not imply acclamation of a divine being. The Aramaic cry *maranatha* ('Lord, come') expressed the longing of a community which waited in hope for its leader's second coming. For Gentiles, Kyrios or Lord Jesus became a title, referring to Jesus' status. It is 'an acclamation and proclamation'.[13] In the Gentile world, Kyrios was a common address to the gods and it was used of the emperor, a divine being. In the Septuagint, the Greek translation of the Hebrew Bible, Kyrios was a word used of God. Seeing Jesus as the fulfiller of Hebrew prophecies, it would have been easy to apply the term Kyrios to Jesus. In so doing, the divinity of Jesus was emphasized.

Son of Man

There has perhaps been more discussion of the term 'Son of Man' than of any other title. Although it is the title most commonly put on the lips of Jesus in the Synoptic Gospels, its significance is so uncertain that it is dangerous to draw any conclusions from it about Jesus' self-understanding. Sometimes it is used as a way of speaking of himself. 'The Son of Man has nowhere to lay his head' (Matt. 8.20). At other times, it is used in predictions of his suffering and death. 'He began to teach them that the Son of Man had to undergo great sufferings . . .' (Mark 8.31). The third use is with reference to when 'the Son of Man comes in the glory of his

Father and of the holy angels' (Mark 8.38). This future reference is sometimes interpreted in the light of Daniel 7.

Some scholars, such as the Jewish Geza Vermes, who has concentrated on the study of the Dead Sea Scrolls and who has written also about Jesus and the New Testament, argue 'that there is no evidence whatever, either inside or outside the Gospels, to imply, let alone demonstrate, that the *son of man* was used as a title . . . The only possible, indeed probable, genuine utterances are sayings independent of Daniel 7 in which, in accordance with Aramaic usage, the speaker refers to himself as the *son of man* out of awe, reserve or humility.'[14] Others, such as Conzelmann, think that it was a title, but that its use as such originated in the early Christian community and not with Jesus himself.[15]

Summary

It seems, then, that we have to speak with great caution about the claims that Jesus made for himself. We do not have the evidence to speculate about his self-understanding and it is doubtful whether he used of himself any of the titles applied to him by New Testament writers. It has been suggested above that he believed a new age was dawning, which he was called to proclaim. The cleansing of the Temple, the choice of twelve disciples, the miracles, the welcome to publicans and sinners may be evidence of this belief. He spoke of the boundless generosity of God and called on people to live as children, happy in God's protection and subject to God's rule. Like Martin Luther King, he may have had a premonition of the fate that awaited him.

Christology is an attempt to convey the significance Jesus has for those who believe in him and who through him have discovered new life and a new relationship to God. A particular form of confession of faith is not, however required by Jesus himself, as far as we can reconstruct his life and ministry.

To those who first believed in him he made God present in a new way. They spoke of his being raised by the Father as being similar to the deliverance from Egypt and the revelation at Sinai. The believers read the scriptures in a new light and found in them confirmation of their faith. They applied to Jesus titles drawn from their Jewish heritage. Yet it is clear that there is no single consistent christology in the New Testament. Rather different writers used whatever language they could to convey the significance of Jesus to them. The New Testament does not impose on future generations a single orthodox christology. That comes later when, after the councils of the church, the Emperors hoped to find in Christianity a cohesive faith to bind together their scattered subjects.

2. Christological developments in the Gentile church

As the church became increasingly Gentile, the titles used of Jesus emphasized his divine status. The first Jewish believers saw in him the presence of God and the herald of the kingdom. Gentile Christians spoke of Jesus as 'Son of God' and 'God'. As Gentile Christians emphasized his divinity, so they separated him from Judaism. The christological developments of the councils of the Gentile church may, positively, be seen as authentic developments, attempting to affirm in ways appropriate to their historical circumstances the presence of God in Jesus Christ. They were, negatively, partly responsible for the increasingly condemnatory attitude of Christian teachers and preachers towards Jews and Judaism.

Yet if we accept a historical approach to the creeds, we need not be bound by their formulations and can work towards a christology which is free of negative overtones towards Judaism. The creeds were, as the patristic scholar Frances Young points out, culturally conditioned. Patristic discussion of christology was conducted within the framework of contemporary philosophical discussions. The creeds become problematic, therefore, when they are regarded as an unchangeable expression of Christian belief for all time.

Many of the presuppositions and thought forms of the church fathers are no longer accepted today. For example, to stress the substantive union of Father and Son may be misleading when we think in dynamic terms rather than in terms of substance. Words also have changed their meanings. Terms like 'person' have acquired today a different connotation from their connotation when the creeds were formulated.[16] One effect of these developments has been to focus attention on the divinity of Jesus as the object of Christian worship, rather than on seeing him as the way to the Father. This has served to separate Jesus of Nazareth from his historical Jewish milieu.

If we see the language of the creeds as historically conditioned, this also allows us to see them as expressing the significance of Jesus to those who believe in him, rather than as ontological statements. John

Hick, a philosopher of religion who has done much to question both the traditional Christian understanding of incarnation and the attitude to other faiths, has written: 'It seems reasonable to conclude that the real point and value of incarnational doctrine is not indicative but expressive, not to assert a metaphysical fact but to express a valuation and evoke an attitude.'[17]

Many Christians today do not share the philosophical presuppositions of the church fathers. Critical historical study of the New Testament and Jewish milieu suggests that, unwittingly, the church fathers misread the Gospel evidence. In affirming God's presence in Jesus Christ, I believe I share the underlying affirmation of the fathers and the creeds and stand in the tradition of faith which they proclaimed. I do not, however, feel bound by their formularies. The need is to develop contemporary christologies, and especially one which is truer to the relationship of Judaism and Christianity.

3. A christology for the Jewish–Christian reality

For many people this is too threatening. As the Catholic writer Gregory Baum said ten years ago: 'It is at this point that some Christian theologians get "cold feet". They fear that a radical reinterpretation of the Church's central doctrine might dissolve the gospel altogether.'[18]

Paul van Buren is one of the few writers who is attempting to develop a systematic christology which is free from anti-Judaism. In doing this, he has made two fundamental decisions. The first is that every proper christological statement, however 'high', will make clear that it gives the glory to God the Father. Secondly, every proper christological statement will make clear that it is an affirmation of the covenant between God and Israel.[19]

Many Christians in their emphasis on Jesus Christ seem almost to forget the Father. As John Bowden, a critical theologian who is Editor of SCM Press, has written in a recent study: 'The symbols of Jesus and the Christ . . . occupy too prominent a place in Christianity. They have accumulated too much power; so much power indeed that in many contexts the figure of Jesus has come to eclipse that of God.'[20] As a result, Jesus is used to separate Christians from other believers in God. He is the way to God, understood as Father (a Jewish concept), but there are other understandings of God which may enrich us. He is a symbol of the ultimate, not the ultimate himself. We cannot dispense with symbols, but other symbols may illuminate other aspects of the one divine reality. Very particularly, an approach which seems to see Jesus as the whole of God rather than the key to God aggravates the differences between Jews and Muslims on the one hand and Christians on the other. If we remember that in our praise of Jesus Christ we are glorifying his Father, then our christology need not separate us so sharply.

Indeed, we have to find room in our theology to see meaning in the Jewish rejection of the claims made for Jesus. That most Jews have rejected the claims of Jesus is perhaps a warning to Christians not so to concentrate on Jesus that they neglect the Father. Christians are perhaps also cautioned not to make an idol of their religion nor to claim a monopoly of the truth.

Equally, we need to recognize that all that we say of Jesus affirms his relationship to his own people. If he was indeed a faithful son of the covenant, then he confirms the truths and values of the covenant of Sinai. Those who are seeking to develop a christology for the Jewish–Christian reality wish to affirm that – to echo the title of a book by the influential Scottish theologian Donald Baillie[21] – 'God is in Christ' without denying that God is with his people Israel.[22] To do this requires careful consideration of the relationship of the two covenants, to which we shall turn in the next chapter.

But a refashioned christology has not only to move away from traditional christocentrism and exclusivity. It has to grapple with the continuing reality of evil. The Jewish witness is a warning to Christians not so to spiritualize salvation that the needs of the world are forgotten. To affirm that Jesus was the Messiah vindicated by God not only seems to invalidate Jewish faith, it also appears to ignore the evil of the world, so horribly revealed at Auschwitz and for which the very Christian teaching of the triumph of the cross must take some blame.

Alice and Roy Eckardt, who have written extensively about the theological impact on Christianity of the Holocaust, distinguish various attempts that have been made to reshape Christian teaching.[23] One is to shift the centre of Christian teaching away from christology and the resurrection. The emphasis, for example, may be placed on Christ's work of opening the covenant to Gentiles. Alternatively, Pawlikowski makes the incarnation central as 'the manifestation of the divine-human nexus'. 'Put somewhat simply,' he writes, 'what ultimately came to be recognized with clarity for the first time through the ministry and person of Jesus was how profoundly integral humanity was to the self-definition of God. This in turn implied that each human person is somehow divine, that he or she somehow shares in the constitutive nature of God. Christ is the theological symbol that the Church selected to try to express this reality.'[24]

A second possibility is to continue to speak of the resurrection as a divine event that happened, but to try to rid it of its triumphalist feeling. Jacobus (Coos) Schoneveld, the General Secretary of the International Council of Christians and Jews, for example, says: 'The resurrection means the vindication of Jesus as a Jew, as a person who was faithful to the Torah, as a martyr who participated in Jewish martyrdom for the sanctification of God's Name. What else can this mean than the validation of the Torah and vindication of the Jewish people as God's beloved people?'[25]

A third possibility is to say that the resurrection of Jesus has not yet occurred, but is still an event in the future. For to say that it has happened and that 'evil has been defeated' ignores the continuing reality of pain and wickedness. Rosemary Ruether writes: 'The crucifixion of the Messiah by the unredeemed forces of history cannot be overcome by the proclamation of Easter and then transformed into a secret triumph. Easter gives no licence to vilify those who cannot "see it". Indeed, we must see that Easter does not cancel the crucifixion at all. There is no triumph in history. Easter is hope against what remains the continuing reality of the cross.'[26]

The resurrection is then the affirmation of faith that the way of self-giving love will be victorious – it is an anticipatory or 'proleptic' celebration. In the Fourth Gospel, the moment of Jesus' death is also the moment of his glorification (John 12.23). The evangelist also speaks of him 'being lifted up' (John 12.32) – a word that implies both his being lifted up on the cross and his being exalted to glory. Easter faith, therefore, is a commitment in hope to follow the way of Jesus and with him to identify with the victims of history. It is not, as so often Christian celebration of Easter seems to suggest, just an objective event.

Later, as we seek to reflect on the Shoah, we shall return to the question of God suffering. Perhaps because our picture of divine power has been wrong, we have misinterpreted the death and resurrection of Jesus in a triumphalist way and this is bound up with Christian anti-Judaism. Jesus on the cross calls us in compassion to identify ourselves with all victims of human cruelty and to follow his way of self-giving love. That suffering and self-giving love is, I believe, of the nature of God and wherever it is expressed, there is God. *Ubi caritas, ibi Deus* ('where love is, there is God').

It is modern hymn writers, perhaps more than theologians, who point us towards a new christology.

To quote first from a song by Sydney Carter,

> 'The poor of the world are my body,' he said,
> 'To the end of the world they shall be . . .'
> 'My body will hang on the cross of the world
> Tomorrow,' he said, 'and today.'[27]

There is a similar appeal in Timothy Rees' hymn 'O Crucified Redeemer':

> Today we see thy Passion
>   spread open to our gaze;
> The crowded street, the country lane,
>   its Calvary displays.
>
> Wherever love is outraged,
>   wherever hope is killed,
> Where man still wrongs his brother man,
>   thy Passion is fulfilled.[28]

6

An Eternal Covenant

The claim that God's covenant with Israel is still valid is becoming a commonplace of church statements on Christian–Jewish relations. How the covenants are related remains a matter of debate. Some speak of a single covenant into which Gentiles have been admitted through Jesus Christ; others speak of two parallel covenants. In my view, there are difficulties with both positions. Whilst there is a special relationship of Christianity to Judaism, the theological question is similar to that posed by the existence of other world religions. Is God's concern and saving love confined to those who are Christian? To accept that God's covenant with Israel is still valid implies that the answer is 'no'. Yet much liturgical and ecclesiastical practice still assumes that Christianity has a monopoly of truth and has replaced Israel in God's purposes.

Church statements

The statements of several denominations from different parts of the world, as we have seen, affirm the continuing validity of God's covenant with Israel, even if this is seldom obvious in the church's preaching and practice. A few examples will serve to illustrate current official teaching. The Second Vatican Council, in the decree *Nostra Aetate*, affirmed that 'God holds the Jews most dear for the sake of their Fathers; He does not repent of the gifts He makes or of the call He issues – such is the witness of the Apostle.'[1] The Diocese of Cleveland, USA, in guidelines drawn up in 1979, quoting this passage, precedes it with these words: 'Our respect and regard for Judaism, therefore, is not for an ancient relic of the distant past. It is God himself who made the Jewish people his own and gave them a divine and irrevocable vocation.'[2]

The same view has been affirmed by several Protestant churches. The churches in the Netherlands, for example, in 1981 declared: 'The promises which the God of Abraham, Isaac, and Jacob has made to the Jewish people have never been revoked by their God, who is our God, too. Nor did God ever recall the covenant which He, through Moses, had made with them. We Christians call this covenant – by a term which has occasioned much misunderstanding – the "old covenant". This covenant was not abolished or replaced by the "new covenant" in and through the coming of Jesus Christ. Jesus himself states emphatically the fulfilment of the Law and Prophets (Matt. 5.17). Paul wrote about those Jews who did not recognize the Messiah in Jesus, "As regards election they are beloved for the sake of their forefathers. For the gifts and the call of God are irrevocable" (Rom. 11.28). The apostle even emphasizes the advantage of Jews, for they "are entrusted with the oracles of God" (Rom. 3.2).'[3] The 1982 Statement of the Texas Conference of Churches likewise declares: 'We acknowledge with both respect and reverence that Judaism is a living faith and that Israel's call and covenant are valid and operative today. We reject the position that the covenant between the Jews and God was dissolved with the coming of Christ. Our conviction is grounded in the teaching of Paul in Romans, chapters 9–11, that God's gift and call are irrevocable. The Jewish people today possess their own unique call and mission before God and their covenant.'[4] The Bishops of the Anglican Communion at the 1988 Lambeth Conference agreed that 'We firmly reject any view of Judaism which sees it as a living fossil, simply superseded by Christianity' and went on to refer to Romans 9–11.[5]

Traditional teaching

These statements may not appear very striking until they are contrasted with the traditional view that is sometimes labelled 'supersessionist' or 'the theory of replacement'. Those Christians who have claimed to have taken over the promises of the covenant have often adopted an anti-Jewish stance that has prepared the way for horrific attacks upon Jews. The new view, therefore, is a vital part of efforts to purge Christian teaching of anti-Judaism.

The dominant view in the church has been that the new covenant replaced the old covenant. It was claimed that with the resurrection of Jesus, the church, the 'new Israel' or 'new people of God' became the heir to the promises made to Abraham and the patriarchs long ago. By its rejection of Jesus, Israel had shown itself unfaithful and had reneged on the covenant. In punishment, God destroyed the holy city of Jerusalem and banished the Jewish people from the Promised Land. The parable of the vineyard was taken to support this teaching. The vineyard's tenants are warned that after they kill the owner's son, he will come and put the tenants to death and give the vineyard to others (Mark 12.9).

In mediaeval teaching, the survival of the Jews, with their sufferings and disabilities, was sometimes regarded as a warning of the dangers of apostasy. At other times, they were regarded as a 'fossil' community, which has no continuing purpose or significance once Christ had come. This was illustrated for me at a conference in India, to which a rabbi friend had come. One of the Indian Christian students came up to him, and said how pleased he was to meet a living example of an 'ancient religion which he had read about'.

An eternal covenant

The view that God has rejected his covenant with Israel is unsatisfactory for several reasons. It calls in question God's trustworthiness and faithfulness to his promises. It ignores the continuing spiritual fecundity of Israel and the faithfulness of the Jewish people. It is based on a misreading of Jesus' attitude to the Torah and perhaps also on a misunderstanding of the teaching of Paul.

God's covenant with Israel is eternal, because it is based on God's gracious choice of his people and his rescuing of them from the land of Egypt. A response is called for, but God's promise is not conditional. If it were, then justification is by works – the very error of which Christians so often accuse Jews. If God is thought to be capricious or the covenant conditional, then Christians' own confidence in God's faithfulness is undermined. The character of God is consistent – a God who shows steadfast love and who again and again calls his children back to his loving care. 'If God is not faithful to His people,' asks Paul van Buren, 'if He does not stand by His covenant with Israel, why should we think that He will be any more faithful to His Gentile church?'[6]

Further, throughout the centuries, many Jews have remained faithful to the covenant and obedient to Torah. Their faithfulness witnesses to the continuing validity of the covenant. Through the centuries the religious life of the Jewish people has continued to develop. The link with the Promised Land has also never been lost.

Jesus and the law

The 'replacement theory' does not do justice to scripture. According to Matthew, Jesus says, 'Do not suppose that I have come to abolish the Law and the prophets; I did not come to abolish, but to complete. I tell you this: so long as heaven and earth endure, not a letter, not a stroke, will disappear from the Law until all that must happen has happened' (or 'before all that it stands for is achieved') (Matt. 5.17, NEB). Jesus, it has been suggested above, was faithful to the Torah. 'We have found,' E. P. Sanders writes, 'one instance in which Jesus, in effect, demanded transgression of the law: the demand to the man whose father had died. Otherwise the material in the Gospels reveals no transgression by Jesus . . . On the other hand, there is clear evidence that he did not consider the Mosaic dispensation to be final or absolutely binding . . . This attitude almost certainly sprang from his conviction that the new age was at hand . . . It was Jesus' sense of living at the turn of the ages which allowed him to think that the Mosaic law was not final and absolute. The disciples did not gain the impression that the Mosaic dispensation was valueless and had already passed away . . . Nothing which Jesus said or did which bore on the law led his disciples after his death to disregard it. This great fact, which overrides all others, sets a definite limit to what can be said about Jesus and the law.'[7]

In the new age, the position of Gentiles was also to be changed. It has been said that the question of the Gentiles was the crucial question which confronted Judaism.[8] There was a considerable Jewish mission to the Gentiles. Paul found his most receptive audience amongst the God-fearers. It seems that most Jews agreed that in the last days Gentiles would be admitted to the kingdom, but were uncertain on what terms. Biblical passages were vague and it was not clear whether Gentiles had to become proselytes.[9] The argument in the early church seems to have centred on this point – not on whether Gentiles could be admitted to the church, but on the terms of admission. Paul insisted that it was not necessary for Gentiles to observe the Torah.

Paul and Judaism

Questions about the right way to interpret Paul's attitude to the Law turn largely on whom he was addressing, especially in the Letter to the Galatians. The churches of Galatia were mainly made up of Gentiles (4.8). Some of them were deserting Paul and listening to those who told them that they must incorporate some elements of Jewish ritual observance, especially circumcision (5.6). 'The importance of these circumstances for understanding the letter as a whole,' writes the American scholar John Gager in his important book *The Origins of Anti-Semitism*, 'can scarcely be over-emphasized. Jews and Judaism are nowhere in the picture. Judaizing, not Judaism, is the issue . . . Paul's sole concern is to defend the status of his Gentile converts as sons of Abraham without first becoming Jews.'[10] Paul insisted that those Gentiles who believed in Jesus Christ were full citizens of the people of God, and did not need to adopt the Torah of Israel.

This same point is made in his letter to the Romans. Paul begins by attacking Jewish 'boasting' – this was the claim that Jews had exclusive access to righteousness and the knowledge of God and that the only hope for Gentiles was to obey Torah. 'The only radical element in his preaching,' says Gager, 'will be that Christ now offers to Gentiles what Israel always claimed to be possible only with the Torah . . . Not that the Torah ceases to be "useful" for Jews, but that its significance for Israel has now been replicated for Gentiles through Christ.'[11] Paul insists that doing the Law, not hearing it, is what matters (2.25). Obedient Jews and righteous Gentiles stand on an equal footing (2.13–15). Yet, he takes care to correct any impression that he is undermining the Torah for Jews. 'Circumcision has value, provided you keep the law' (2.25; 3.1; 3.3–8). Chapter 3.9–26 does not invalidate Judaism, but puts Gentiles on an equal basis. 'God is one, and he will put the Jews right with himself on the basis of their faith, and the Gentiles right through their faith' (3.30 TEV/GNB). 'Apart from the Law' (3.21) 'neither asserts nor implies anything in opposition to or against the Torah.'[12]

Paul's purpose is to assert the changed significance of the Torah for those Gentiles who are under Christ. He is attacking Jewish boasting, which denies salvation to Gentiles apart from the Law. God is the God of the Gentiles as well as of the Jews. The Jews are justified not by the possession of the Torah but by obedience to it (2.1–29). Gentiles who previously stood condemned by the Law, now are justified through faith in Jesus Christ (3.22, 26). There are therefore two separate groups whom God will justify on the basis of their faithfulness – Jews who are obedient to the Torah and Gentiles who have faith in Christ. Paul therefore insists that his stress on faith in no way undermines the Law (3.31).[13]

In chapter 4, Paul again attacks boasting. Against the claim that Israel's special position was guaranteed by the promise to Abraham, Paul argues that Abraham was justified before he was circumcised, on the basis of his faith, so that he was the forefather of all who believe. 'Abraham is the spiritual father of all who believe in God and are accepted as righteous by him, even though they are not circumcised. He is also the father of those who are circumcised, not just because they are circumcised, but because they live the same life of faith that our father Abraham lived before he was circumcised' (4.11–12, TEV/GNB).

Bishop Krister Stendahl, the distinguished New Testament scholar who was for a time Moderator of the World Council of Churches' Consultation on the Church and the Jewish People, and others, have argued that in Romans 7, Paul is not talking of his pre-conversion experience nor is he contesting the Law's validity. Rather it is the Gentiles who are the primary focus of his attention. The dilemma of Gentiles before Christ was that any who failed to uphold the entire Torah fell under a curse of condemnation and death (Gal. 3.10; Rom. 5.12–14, 20–21; 7.5). Unlike Jews, they had always been without recourse. Now Jesus Christ sets the Gentiles free from this condemnation (7.25). For Paul identifies himself totally with his Gentile readers and includes himself in their company (cf. Gal. 3.14).[14]

The question that Paul then takes up in Romans 9–11 is: 'Given the constancy of God's righteousness, what are we to make of Israel's refusal to recognize and accept the obvious continuity between God's promise to Abraham and his act of redemption in Christ?' Temporarily God has suspended Israel's privileges as God's chosen people. Israel had failed in its pursuit of righteousness based on the Torah (9.31; 10.3); its zeal for God was unenlightened (10.2); Israel had been disobedient (11.30–32); and finally, 'a hardening has come upon a part of Israel' (11.25). Furthermore a fundamental component of Israel's self-understanding, the privileged relation to God provided by the Mosaic covenant, has been permanently revoked. And yet Paul goes to great lengths to deny certain inferences that were already being drawn in his own time and which have served as the traditional view of Paul. At three points in chapter 11 he denies that Israel has been rejected by God. In 11.2, he states simply that God has not rejected the people whom he foreknew. In 11.11, he denies that their stumbling leads to their fall. 'By no means!' is his reply. And in 11.28, he affirms that 'the gifts and the call of God are irrevocable'.[15] It is important also to remember that Paul thought the Second Coming and the completion of God's purposes, which would include the restoration of Israel, was imminent.[16]

Krister Stendahl has also emphasized that the relation of Jews and Christians was Paul's primary concern in the letter to the Romans rather than 'justification by faith'. Stendahl notes that in chapters 9–11, Paul never says that Israel will accept Jesus as Messiah at the time of God's kingdom, but that 'all Israel will be saved' (11.26). On the extended discussion in 10.17–11.36, he comments that Paul fails there to mention the name of Jesus Christ. Perhaps most significant is the suggestion, which he does not develop, that Paul's thinking on the relationship of Christianity and Judaism may be seen as anticipating the view of Christianity developed in a line of Jewish thinking stretching from Maimonides to Rosenzweig: 'Christianity . . . is seen as the conduit of Torah, for the declaration of both monotheism and the moral order to the Gentiles.'[17] Lloyd Gaston, who is Professor of New Testament at Vancouver University, also says: 'Paul's major theological concern I take to be the justification of the legitimacy of the Gentile mission before the end.'[18] If Paul was critical of fellow-Jews for not recognizing God's new dispensation, he does not argue from this failure that God had rejected those Jews who remained obedient to the Torah.

If Gaston and others are right, Paul does not attack the Torah as such, but its imposition upon Gentile believers. Gaston sharply disagrees with those like Rosemary Ruether[19] or E. P. Sanders[20] who have said that, for Paul, Torah and Christ are mutually exclusive categories. In Gaston's view, Paul's concern was, positively, with the position of the Gentiles. For Paul, Jesus was the fulfilment of God's promises to them. Paul was not telling Jews that they need no longer obey the Torah, as some Jewish opponents wrongly claimed, although he did say that it was obedience to Torah that God required, not its mere possession. He was opposing the attempt to impose Mosaic observances on Gentile converts to Christianity. He did not, Gaston claims, attack the Torah as such.

Yet even if Paul did not attack the Torah as such but its imposition on Gentile converts, inevitably the question was raised why Jewish believers should continue to observe the Torah, if it was not necessary for Gentiles. There seems to have been no convincing answer, as by the end of the first century, in a predominantly Gentile church, not only were Jewish Christians not expected to keep the Law, but Jewish observance itself came under attack. Justin Martyr, in the second century, states that he would accept those who continued to observe the Torah into Christian fellowship, provided they did not seek to convince Gentile Christians to follow the Mosaic Law. He admitted that others rejected the openness of his view. By the fourth century, the church had ruled that it was heretical even for believers of Jewish birth to keep the Law.[21]

The American scholar Terrence Callan, in his book *Forgetting the Root*, argues that it was the decision by the Church that Gentiles need not keep the Jewish Law which led to the emergence of Christianity as a separate religion. He suggests that three positions can be discerned in the early church. There were conservative Jewish Christians who insisted that Gentile converts should observe the Law; there were liberal Jewish Christians who retained a positive view of Judaism, but did not hold that Gentile Christians were required to keep the Law; and Gentile Christians who agreed that Gentiles need not keep the Law. This latter group soon lost sight of the positive place of Judaism in the economy of salvation. They came to a negative view of the Law and held that Jewish Christians and indeed Jews themselves should not observe it.[22]

Such a negative view of the Law has been dominant in the churches through the centuries. It is, as has already been argued, a misunderstanding of the place of Torah in Judaism. The recent writings referred to above suggest also that it does not reflect the teaching of Jesus nor the views of Paul. The new covenant did not set aside the covenant with Israel.

One covenant or two?

If then God's covenant with Israel continues, but, as Christians believe, he has made a new covenant in the blood of Jesus, what is the relationship of these two covenants? The easy answer is that in Jesus the promises of God's covenant with his people Israel are extended to the Gentiles. Such a view would remove the hostility and rivalry between members of the two covenants, but it does not do justice to the differences between the two religions nor allow for Jewish believers in Jesus, who are often treated as an embarrassment by those engaged in Christian–Jewish dialogue.

One covenant

Several writers have discussed this issue. For some there is one covenant into which through Jesus Christ the Gentiles are admitted. Monika Hellwig appears to view the two faith-traditions of Christianity and Judaism as complementary aspects of the same ultimate divine purpose. That eschatological reality must be seen as future, by Christians as well as by Jews. Even for Christians, she says, 'there is an important sense in which Jesus is not yet Messiah . . . What may be expected in the Messianic fulfillment has not yet become manifest in the world.'[23] Messiahship constitutes a mission incumbent upon the entire church of God to realize in history. The one continuous covenant can be described as new after the Christ-event only in the sense that now it embraces both Jews and Gentiles. Jesus has allowed non-Jews to enter the election first bestowed upon the people of Israel.[24]

Paul van Buren also questions Christian claims that Jesus was the Messiah, and sees the church as the community of the Gentiles who have been drawn by the God of the Jews to worship him and make his love known among the nations. Van Buren insists that this does not imply any dilution of the Christian claim that Jesus is the Christ nor of worship of him as Son of God. For those Gentiles who through the Christ-event came for the first time to be drawn into the plan of God, what took place in Jesus could not be understood as merely one episode in the history of salvation. Rather, 'it marked a genuinely new beginning, a step out and beyond the circles of God's covenant with His people, the Jews. But it surely cannot and does not detract from, much less annul, that covenant.'[25]

Roy Eckardt has also insisted that Christianity has not replaced Israel in the drama of human salvation and insists that Israel's divinely determined vocation continues intact into our time. He sees Israel and the church standing in dialectical tension to each other within one covenant. Perhaps the clearest expression of the so-called 'one-covenant' view is expressed by Dr J. Coos Schoneveld. He has written: 'When we look at the Church's life and teaching, has anything been added to the Torah? I have searched for a long time for anything new. In fact nothing new is there, which goes beyond a certain change of emphasis or a certain different nuance in comparison with Jewish teachings of the first century, except that through Jesus the Gentiles have been admitted and the range of the teaching of the Torah has become much wider. What is given in the Torah comes to us Gentiles through Jesus Christ.'[26]

Two covenants

One of the first exponents of the 'two-covenant theory' was the Anglican scholar James Parkes, writing before the Second World War. He was aware of the differences between the two covenants. He interprets the 'Sinai' experience as essentially communal in orientation, while 'Calvary' revolves much more around an understanding of the individual person. 'The highest purpose of God which Sinai reveals to men as community, Calvary reveals to man as an end in himself. The difference between the two events, both of which from the metaphysical standpoint are identical as expressions of the infinite in time, lies in the fact that the first could not be fulfilled but by a brief demonstration of a divine community in action; but the second could not be fulfilled except by a life lived under human conditions from birth to death.'[27] The revelation represented by Calvary did not replace Sinai. On the other hand, Sinai could not simply absorb it and remain unchanged. For Parkes, Judaism and Christianity are inextricably linked together as equals.

Pawlikowski also recognizes the distinctiveness of the two religions. As we have seen, he lays stress on the incarnation. He admits that his christological vision does imply a degree of universalism, but he insists that Judaism 'continues to play a unique and distinctive role in the process of human salvation'. Yet, despite their shared biblical heritage and other similarities, Judaism and Christianity, he says are *essentially distinct religions*, each emphasizing different but complementary aspects of human religiosity'.[28] Amongst the distinct features of Judaism that Pawlikowski mentions are its sense of peoplehood, of community, the belief that no individual can achieve salvation apart from the salvation of the whole human family and its sense of the goodness of creation. It is uncertain, however, whether the differences between the two covenants can be so neatly categorized and whether he allows for the great variety within each religion.

The important point, however, is that he moves away from a 'double covenant' theory to recognize that Judaism and Christianity grew into separate and distinct religions and *that they are equal*. 'The revelation at Sinai stands on an equal footing with the revelation in Jesus.'[29]

The context of world religions

The recognition that Christianity and Judaism had become separate and distinct religions by at the latest the early second century CE, and that each has had its own individual history and development, suggests that their relationship may best be considered in the context of the relationship of world faiths to one another. Both single- and double-covenant theories presume that the Judaeo–Christian tradition has a monopoly of salvation.[30] Further, there is a tendency in discussions based on covenant to take covenant as a given concept. Certainly it is a central way in which biblical writers understand God's dealing with them and their fellow believers, but like 'uniqueness' and 'incarnation' it is a human way of understanding the graciousness of God.

Rosemary Ruether compares the model or 'paradigm' of the resurrection and the Jewish paradigm of the exodus. They are complementary and parallel. She suggests the same might be said of other paradigms of hope within other religions. The Protestant missiologist Gerald Anderson also says that whilst Christianity and Judaism are really different, they are also really complementary. Neither is superior nor final. He goes on to observe that if Christians are able to say this about Judaism, then by a 'domino theory', the same can apply to other religions.[31]

A growing number of Christian writers are recognizing that God's saving activity is present in all religions. This may allow Christians to affirm the integrity of Judaism, especially if Christianity and Judaism are seen as distinct religions, without appearing to minimize Christian claims and without creating a new exclusive Jewish–Christian club.

Single- and double-covenant views tend to assimilate Christianity and Judaism to each other and to disallow the developments of two thousand years. Certainly those two thousand years have been tragic, but Judaism today, deriving from Rabbinic Judaism of the early centuries of the Common Era, and contemporary Christianity have grown and developed over the centuries. The experience and indeed the christological claims of two thousand years cannot just be discounted. Jews and Christians may best be able to give proper esteem to each others' religions as they recognize that they both, as well as other world religions, have a place in the purpose of God.

7

God and Father of All

'A momentous current has begun to flow around and through the Christian Church,' writes Wilfred Cantwell Smith, whose writings on the theology of religions have been very influential. 'It is a current which, although we are only beginning to be aware of it, is about to become a flood that could sweep us quite away unless we can through greatly increased consciousness of its flow and direction learn to swim in its special and mighty surge.'[1] The current, becoming a flood, to which he refers is the increasing pressure on Christians and indeed people of all faiths to become aware of and cope with a religiously plural world, 'which, of course, is the only world there is'.[2]

This flood has occasioned numerous dialogue meetings and a large body of literature about the Christian attitude to other faiths. A growing number of Christians are rejecting the exclusive attitudes that claim for the church a monopoly of truth. These views were predominant in the last century and indeed have been so throughout the history of the church, in so far as the relationship with other religions was given consideration. The phrase *extra ecclesiam nulla salus* (outside the church there is no salvation) typified the general view.

There are several reasons why this view is now brought into question.

The biblical material is itself ambiguous

Besides the exclusive passages in which Baal-worship and idolatry are denounced, there are other passages which suggest that God is concerned for all nations. The covenant which God made with Noah after the flood (Gen. 9.8–17) is understood as a universal covenant of God with all people, prior to the particular covenant with the people of Israel. The prophet Amos declares that neighbouring nations, such as Edom and Moab, are judged by God, as well as Judah and Israel (Amos 1 and 2). In different parts of Isaiah, God was recognized to be active in this history of other nations:

> The Assyrian! He is the rod that I wield in my anger,
> and the staff of my wrath is in his hand.
> I send him against a godless nation . . . (10.5)

Cyrus is called 'the Lord's anointed', whom God has chosen to subdue the nations. God says to him, 'I will go before you and level the swelling hills' (45.1–2). In Malachi 1.11, the Lord of Hosts says: 'From furthest east to furthest west my name is great among the nations. Everywhere fragrant sacrifice and pure gifts are offered in my name, for my name is great among the nations.' This may mean that even now God is honoured by the worship of Gentiles.[3] Besides prophecies of the destruction of the nations, there is also the hope that they too will at the end-time come to worship the God of Israel. 'In those days, when ten men from nations of every language pluck up courage, they shall pluck the robe of a Jew and say, "We will go with you because we have heard that God is with you"' (Zech. 8.23 cf. Isa. 45.14).

In the New Testament, Jesus said that Gentiles would share in the kingdom of God (Matt 8.11) and, in the parable of the sheep and the goats, be judged on the same basis as Jews (Matt. 25.31). Peter told Cornelius: 'I see God has no favourites, but that in every nation, the man who is godfearing and does what is right is acceptable to him' (Acts 10.34). There is a universalism in the letters to the Colossians and Ephesians.[4] This strand needs to be weighed against the exclusive claims in the Fourth Gospel where Jesus says, 'No man come to the Father but through me' (John 14.6).[5]

The Christian tradition is not monochrome

The dominant view amongst Christians in the last century was that all others were perishing in darkness. The great missionary movement sprang from deep love and concern for the 'benighted', although some missionaries pioneered the study of the scriptures of other religions. A glance at the section on 'Foreign Missions' in *The*

Methodist School Hymnal, published early in this century, gives a flavour of popular Christian teaching:

> A cry, as of pain,
> Again and again,
> Is borne o'er the deserts and wide-spreading main:
> God and Father of All.
> A cry from the lands that in darkness are lying,
> A cry from the hearts that in sorrow are sighing.
>> It comes unto me;
>> It comes unto thee:
>> O what – O what shall the answer be (no. 492).

> I often think of heathen lands,
>> Far away, far away,
> Where many a pagan temple stands,
>> Far away, far away:
> And there each hapless child is led
> To bow to idol gods his head,
> Whilst many a muttered charm is said,
>> Far away, far away (no. 494).

Yet there has been a minority tradition more open to the possibility of truth being present beyond Christendom. The second-century Christian apologist Justin Martyr hoped to meet Plato in heaven, and St Augustine spoke of Christianity being as old as the hills. In the Middle Ages, Nicholas of Cusa, who was a mathematician and an influential philosopher as well as a cardinal, suggested that behind all religious differences, there was one universal religion – even if it did include belief in the Trinity and the Mass. In the seventeenth century, Robert de Nobili, an Italian Jesuit of good family who settled in Madurai, started wearing the ochre robe of a Hindu sannyasi. When he taught the Christian faith in South India, he said: 'The law which I preach is the law of the true God, which from ancient times was by his command proclaimed in these countries by sannyasis and saints.'[6]

An exclusive view is inconsistent with the God revealed by Jesus Christ

A growing number of Christians cannot believe that the God of love revealed by Jesus Christ would create children who were destined for damnation, just because they did not believe in Jesus Christ, of whom they had never heard. To suggest, as Paul does in Rom. 9.20, that God acts like a potter who can do what he likes with the clay and make some vessels for destruction and others for glory is to make God less moral than our highest insights. A loving God surely wills that all people may be saved. This is agreed by most leading twentieth-century theologians, although they disagree as to whether some souls for ever resist the love of God.[7]

Various attempts have been made to reconcile the belief that God wills all people to be saved and the evidence that some 'non-Christians' reflect the grace of God, with the dogma that outside the church there is no salvation. Fr Bede Griffiths, for example, a Catholic with a deep appreciation of Hinduism and whose ashram in South India attracts many Hindu and Christian visitors, in his early book *Christian Ashram* (1966) developed St Thomas Aquinas' teaching that it was possible for those who lived before Christ to be saved. Bede Griffiths argued, following Fr Daniélou's book *Holy Pagans of the Old Testament*, that the cosmic covenant of God with all people contained implicitly the revelation of God's saving purpose in Christ. Those saved under the cosmic covenant were saved 'by their implicit faith in Christ and were therefore properly members of the Church of Christ'.[8] Bede Griffiths spoke also of the hidden call of grace, 'which comes to every man secretly in every religious or irreligious state'.[9]

A rather similar ploy is to speak of 'baptism by desire'. This presumes that good people of other faiths would have been baptized if they had had the opportunity and so may be counted as members of the church. Another way, used by the great Catholic theologian Karl Rahner, is to speak of 'anonymous Christians'. 'Christianity,' he wrote in 1961, 'does not simply confront the member of an extra-Christian religion as a mere non-Christian but as someone who can and must be regarded in this or that respect as an anonymous Christian.'[10] But besides being patronizing, this approach may mask the real differences of belief between committed members of the great religions.

These charitable suggestions in fact show that the supposition that there is no salvation outside the church is unacceptable. As John Hick has argued, a shift is needed from a Ptolemaic theological viewpoint, which puts Christianity at the centre and to which all other religions must relate. Instead, a Copernican viewpoint is required in which God is at the centre around whom all religions revolve.[11]

Personal contact with people of other faiths

As more Christians have met and got to know devout adherents of other religions, they have recognized that their adverse opinions of these faiths were prejudiced and ill founded. Charles de Foucauld (1858–1916), the inspirer of the Little Brothers of Jesus, was for a time an officer in the French army in Algeria. He was roused from his then dissolute life and conventional religion by the Muslims on both sides of the conflict stopping fighting at the time of prayer. This is how M. M. Preminger describes the scene:

> The skirmish continued for a good half hour, with Foucauld calling at last for fresh ammunition supplies. There was no response from his own Arabs who had taken cover with the pack animals. Furious, Foucauld galloped back to read the riot act to his men – only to find them prostrating themselves in prayer . . . On the opposite hillside, too, the firing had stopped. At the risk of being shot like sitting ducks, the Uled Sidi Sheikh (snipers) had emerged from cover, turned their backs to the sunset and bowed down to the east . . . Allahu akbar. A strange silence filled the little wadi, a stillness that reminded Foucauld of the awesome quiet of Nancy Cathedral in his boyhood days when he still believed in God. That silence, in fact, had meant to the boy that he was indeed in the presence of God. He had laughed at himself since for such mawkish credulity, but he did not laugh now. These Arabs took God seriously. They had stopped fighting because it was time to pray . . . They had exposed themselves to possible massacre to prostrate themselves before their God, refused to neglect prayer even in the face of the enemy.

The experience was to remain with Charles de Foucauld as a vital factor in his conversion to a deep Christian faith – later expressed in self-giving compassion for Islam.[12]

As a student at Madras Christian College, I used to help at a Leprosy clinic. I usually walked there with another Christian student and a Muslim student, but the doctor at the centre was a devotee of Shiva. We were united, however, in our care for those who were ill. Nor will I forget visiting a home for the dying at Varanasi run by the Ramakrishna Order and in particular the radiant goodness of the monk who showed me round. Like other Christians, I have been privileged to meet holy people of other faiths, such as Otto Frank, the father of Anne Frank whose diary is world-famous, or the Dalai Lama, and such experiences make it impossible to confine God's sanctifying grace just to the Christian church.

Other scriptures are inspiring

In a similar way, a growing number of Christians have read and studied the scriptures of other religions. Despite the unfamiliarity, they have found them deeply moving and inspiring. I recall visiting Fr Murray Rogers' Ashram in India. As a passage was read from the Upanishads (part of the Hindu scriptures) before the biblical readings, I realized that they too could be for me the Word of God.

In his *Alive to God* Kenneth Cragg, much of whose life has been devoted to the study of Islam, has indicated the possibility of Christian prayer being enriched by Muslim devotion. 'Praise may still unite where dogma requires to scrutinize. The one need not always wait for the other . . . The mercies of God in the different fields of prophet and Messiah, of revelation and Scriptures and their institutional issue into faiths – in dispute and contention as these are – still have mutual features we must be careful not to miss. The rule of God, the instrumentality of men, the moral of history, the care of time, the reckoning with death are among them.'[13] *The Oxford Book of Prayer* contains prayers from the religions of the world.

Each year many people of all religions share in the Week of Prayer for World Peace. A large number of Christians have been helped in meditation by teachings deriving from Eastern religious traditions. Experience confirms for a growing number of Christians that God is the source of inspiration in the scriptures and devotions of other faiths.

New Testament claims for Jesus

At any meeting where the subject of the relationship of Christianity to other faiths is discussed, someone is sure to quote the words 'No man cometh to the Father but through me' (John 14.6). Critical scholarship has made clear that the words of Jesus quoted in the Fourth Gospel should not be treated as his actual words. Equally important, although claims to unique authority were implicit in Jesus' teaching, historically at least, christological claims in the New

Testament have to be treated with caution. As I suggested above,[14] many New Testament scholars now recognize that Jesus' own message centred on the kingdom of God rather than on himself. Further, traditional understandings of the doctrine of incarnation are being re-examined.[15] Some writers suggest that overmuch emphasis on Jesus has obscured the fact that Jesus leads us to the Father, the one God of all humankind.

A new relationship

All these points are, of course, matters of discussion and there is much debate on the relationship of Christianity to other world religions: but there is a widespread move from rejecting other religions as 'godless' to seeing that they have a place in God's purposes. Whilst Christians affirm that for them God's definitive self-revelation is in Jesus Christ and that he is of universal significance, they can recognize that other religions have their own validity.

Dr Robert Runcie, Archbishop of Canterbury, in a lecture in memory of Sir Francis Younghusband, founder of the World Congress of Faiths, said: 'The central message of the Christian gospel is a message of love, love poured out in the complete self-giving of God in His Son for the sake of all life and creation. For the Christian this is firm and fundamental – it is not negotiable. Nonetheless, Christians recognize that other faiths reveal other aspects of God which may enrich and enlarge our Christian understanding . . . We will have to abandon any narrowly conceived Christian apologetic, based on a sense of superiority and an exclusive claim to truth.'[16]

There has been a considerable movement of thought amongst some Christians, but the breakthrough still widely needed is to recognize that all the world religions have a place in God's purposes and that each has a message to give to the world. We are beginning to see that each religion has a vital contribution to make to our awareness of truth and of spiritual values. Bishop George Appleton, whose worldwide ministry has involved him in deep contact with people of other faiths, expressed this in a sermon at the Fortieth Anniversary Conference of the World Congress of Faiths, when he said: 'Each religion has a mission, a gospel, a central affirmation. Each of us needs to enlarge on the gospel which he has received without wanting to demolish the gospel of others . . . We can enlarge and deepen our initial and basic faith by the experience and insights of people from other religions and cultures, without disloyalty to our own commitment.'[17] This new understanding is to recognize that each major religion is a channel of and response to God's grace.

This is not to pretend that all religions are the same, but to recognize that the unique witness of each tradition may contribute to a richer whole that has yet to be grasped. The American Catholic R. E. Whitson put it like this: 'Each of the world religions is unique and universal: unique in that the core of each is a distinct central experience – not to be found elsewhere – and universal in that this core experience is of supreme significance for all men. It is the ability of a tradition of religious experience to speak to other men that calls us to recognize it as a world religion.'[18] Each religion derives from a core experience such as the covenant at Sinai or the Buddha's enlightenment. This is the hub of the wheel. The doctrines, rituals and practices relate like the spokes of a wheel. In this sense each religion is unique and an organic whole. Yet its central message is relevant to all people, as there is an inherent universality about the claim to truth which each religion makes. Some Christians, therefore, as Gordian Marshall puts it, 'are beginning to recognize a need to work on an understanding of Jesus, which says that the presence of Christians in the world can be a blessing for the whole world *without* the whole world being Christian'.[19] In a similar way, Kenneth Cragg, speaking of Islam, says: 'What has authority for some of the human race must have relevance for all. As a "mercy to the worlds", Muhammad and the Qur'an cannot well be confined within Islam, nor their significance withheld from those who do not assent to its beliefs.'[20] Indeed, in 1931 the great German scholar Rudolf Otto said: 'No religion should die before it has had the opportunity of uttering its last and most profound word.'[21]

Such an approach, arising out of the experience of dialogue, awakens the expectation of convergence, that as religions meet and share, so they will gradually come closer together. As Whitson has said, this is not something that can be argued for so much as felt. It springs from a deep conviction that there is One God who is Father of all, whose love is truly universal. To recognize the mutuality of religions is to see that each has a place in God's purposes and that each has a vital contribution to make to men and women's spiritual progress. It is to see a theological significance in other faiths. This approach is also aware of the limitations of human knowledge and of credal statements and that any language about the Holy One points to a reality beyond description.[22]

The significance of Jesus

Such an approach also means that Jesus Christ is seen in a new light, although not, as critics suggest, in a way that diminishes him, but in a way that gives him a more universal significance. Towards the end of his years in India, the missionary C. F. Andrews said that through his deep contact with members of other faiths, 'Christ has become not less central but more central and universal: not less divine to me, but more so because more universally human.'[23]

If God is one, then the God revealed in Jesus Christ is the one God of all people. The American theologian Schubert Ogden wrote: 'The New Testament sense of the claim "only in Jesus Christ" is not that God is only to be found in Jesus and nowhere else, but that the only God who is to be found anywhere – though he is to be found everywhere – is the God who is made known in the word that Jesus speaks and is.'[24] In Jesus, the reality of God as loving Father is made known and wherever signs of God's activity are recognized, it will be one and the same God who is seen to be at work.

In and through Jesus, I believe that in his mercy I have been met by God. He is the window (or 'disclosure situation', to use a phrase of Ian Ramsey, a former Bishop of Durham) for me on to ultimate reality. God will not be other than he is revealed to be in Jesus, but my grasp of that revelation is always inadequate and in need of correction. I appreciate that for the Muslim, the window on to reality is the Qur'an and for the Jew it is the Torah. I see no value in arguing which window gives the better view. Rather in sharing what we see, we each grow in our appreciation of the divine splendour. As I learn from others I see new riches in Jesus Christ, and several members of other faiths have told me of the inspiration that Jesus has been to them. Christians worship God through Jesus Christ, and his promise is to lead us to the Father of all.

8

Dialogue or Mission?

As the World Day of Prayer for Peace at Assisi came to an end, the Imam of the Rome Mosque said to me that the day affirmed 'the validity of all true religions'. Whatever their differences, members of the world religions had been together as prayers from each tradition were offered. The assumption was that each religion addressed one and the same divine reality.

This recognition that each religion has a place in God's purposes and is a community of faith implies a relationship of dialogue and co-operation instead of a missionary stance whereby one religion tries to win over the adherents of another religion.

Dialogue

Dialogue is a word which is now very commonly used, but it may have different meanings. Dialogue occurs at many levels. For some it is a new experience to meet each other on a friendly basis. As a window cleaner said when he first cleaned the windows at the Council of Christians and Jews offices, 'I've never seen Jews and Christians together before'. Much dialogue is intended to promote community understanding and neighbourliness. It can help us to appreciate another's point of view. After attending a peace education workshop at Neve Shalom, an inter-faith community and school for peace in Israel, a young Jewish participant wrote to his Arab counsellor, 'Now, when I hear news of demonstrations or strikes I consider carefully the stark facts from a different angle and try to understand the motive behind the action and the emotions which produce such events.'[1]

Diana Eck, who is Moderator of the World Council of Churches' Sub-Unit for Dialogue, has distinguished six forms of dialogue. The

first is parliamentary-style dialogue. She traces this back to the
1893 World Parliament of Religions and sees it carried forward by
the international inter-faith organizations, such as the New York
based Temple of Understanding. Secondly, there is institutional
dialogue, such as the regular meetings between representatives of
the Vatican and IJCIC (The International Jewish Committee for
Interreligious Consultation). Thirdly, there is theological dialogue, which takes seriously the questions and challenges posed by
people of other faiths. Fourthly, dialogue in community or the
dialogue of life is the search for good relationships in ordinary life.
Spiritual dialogue is the attempt to learn from other traditions of
prayer and meditation. Lastly, there is inner dialogue, which is
'that conversation that goes on within ourselves in any other form
of dialogue'.[2]

In dialogue there is an openness to and acceptance of the other.
It takes time to build trust and to deepen relationships. Very
easily, we find ourselves imposing our presuppositions on the
conversation. Christians for example often assume that Muslims
really adopt a critical attitude to the Qur'an similar to that
common amongst Christians.[3] We have to learn to enter another
world that may seem alien and has different presuppositions. We
have to allow our deepest convictions to be questioned. Some
Buddhists, for example, will question deeply-held Christian
assumptions about God and the self.[4] It is important for those
venturing into dialogue to be secure in their own faith. They need
to beware of becoming marginalized in or alienated from their own
religious tradition. Dialogue needs also to be of equals, that is to
say of those with similar levels of scholarship and study.

At its deepest dialogue will raise questions of truth. Rabbi Dr
Norman Solomon, Director of the Centre for the Study of Judaism
and Jewish–Christian relations at Selly Oak, Birmingham, said in
his inaugural lecture: 'Dialogue admits of degrees: there is dialogue which is of value though it does not reach deep. Much of the
dialogue between Jews and Christians is a matter of simply
learning to be nice to each other, trying a little to understand what
the other is doing, co-operating in social endeavour . . . Many
ordinary Jews or Christians lack the skills necessary to engage in a
deeper, theological dialogue, and are rightly wary of setting their
faith at risk in a confusing enterprise. Yet the heart of dialogue is
in talk together of theologians of both faiths, for it is they whose

concern is with the meaning of life at its deepest level and it is they who translate from the doctrinal formula to the underlying reality.'[5]

Dialogue does not necessarily produce agreement and, if it is a search for truth, there is no desire for easy compromise. Sometimes it makes clearer where essential differences lie, exposing the various presuppositions or views of the world with which partners in dialogue are operating. Sometimes it can be painful. The American Jewish writer Dr Eugene Borrowitz has said: 'Only by directly confronting our deepest differences can we come to know one another fully. Despite risks, inter-religious discussion needs at times to be inter-religious debate. That is one way it shows its conviction that truth is ultimately one.'[6]

Mission

Dialogue is a serious search for truth, but it does suppose that no one religion has a monopoly of truth. This is why dialogue is incompatible with mission. Attempts by some Christians to convert Jews imperil the search for understanding and a new relationship.

A senior Orthodox Rabbi who was driving me to a meeting said as we set out, 'I've always understood that your religious duty is to convert me and that my religious duty is not to be converted.' After that we talked deeply on many matters during our journey. Many Jews, understandably, are not so secure and relaxed on the subject. To feel the other person does not accept you as you are but wants to change you inhibits relaxed and intimate conversation. I remember a Buddhist monk saying at the end of a World Congress of Faiths conference, that it was the first time that Christians had spoken with him, rather than at him. The missionary assumption also reawakens memories of centuries of Christian superiority and oppression.

Jews resent the active and well-financed missionary groups, often based in the USA, which harass some of the Jewish community. Their methods are felt to be often dishonest and aggressive. The Jewish community has an understandable insecurity, not just because of the past, but because in most European countries, Jews are a small minority. Further, for demographic reasons and because of 'marrying out', most European Jewish communities are decreasing. The decline is not because there are many conversions to Christianity. Yet there are some often highly publicized ones. In the USA, the position is rather different, as the Jewish community is larger and it is a society used to vigorous religious competition.

Few question the right of individuals freely to change from one religion to another. The deep Jewish dislike of organized Christian missionary activity, however, seems to be because it perpetuates age-old Christian attitudes to Judaism and calls in question whether the new relationship is deeply rooted. Attempts to convert Jews seem to deny affirmations that God's covenant with Israel continues and that the Jews remain a people of God. Some see missionary activity as more evil and insidious than Hitler's attack on the Jewish world. That sought the physical destruction of Judaism, whereas missionary activity seeks its spiritual destruction. For, if missionary activity were successful, presumably all Jews would become Christians and Judaism would disappear (although some Christians might say it had been fulfilled).

A rabbi, in a response to Christian missionary activity, said this: 'I am conscious that we meet between two festivals not ordained by Torah: the festival of Channukah, which reminds us there was a time when an attempt was made to destroy Judaism, and Purim, a festival which reminds us (should we ever forget) that there was a time when an attempt was made to destroy Jews. The season is thus singularly appropriate for a consideration of a Jewish response to Christian missionary activity, for the Jewish experience of Christian mission has been an all too often repeated journey from Channukah to Purim. When Christianity failed to wean the Jew from his Judaism, his own "benighted" nature made him fair game for those who through religious zeal or for baser motives preferred him dead. As the historian in Landzman's *Shoah* so succinctly described the process: "You may not live here as Jews" became "you may not live here" and finally "you may not live". In Jewish eyes Haman and Christian missionaries have been and continue to be harmful to both the body and the soul of Jews.'[7]

Such a harsh judgment will seem offensive to Christian ears. Allan Brockway makes clear that the growth of Christian missions to Jews in the nineteenth century represented a major change in Christian attitudes to Jews. The desire to convert them was because they too were loved by God and the Christian missionary was to express that love. 'In contrast to earlier centuries, Jews as individuals, as human beings, were not considered degenerate or evil by the missionaries. On the contrary felt love for Jews [*sic*] expressed itself in intense desire to bring them the gospel and thus into the church. Because Christians loved Jews, it was their Christian duty to convince them that the Messiah for whom they waited had already come. Indeed, one argument went, not to preach the gospel to the Jews was antisemitism itself. That this nineteenth- and early twentieth-century attitude towards Jews represented a radical shift from that of preceding generations (when Jews, far from being loved, were actively hated and persecuted) cannot be emphasized enough. Perhaps the shift can be dated from the Enlightenment and then the Emancipation, when Jews were released from the ghettos and encouraged to become part of the general society. As Clermont-Tonnerre, a French philosopher, put it: '"Everything should be denied to the Jews as a nation; everything should be granted to them as individuals."' It therefore became tremendously important that individual Jews be converted to Christianity, while the concept of the Jewish *people* all but entirely vanished from consciousness.'[8] 'For the missionary movement, antisemitism was anathema. Instead, love for "the Jews" was the order of the day.'[9] Although it is hardly surprising that Jews did not perceive conversionism as 'love', when, in the words of a French Protestant statement, 'the aim of general conversion cannot be anything less than the spiritual destruction of Judaism'.[10]

Jews also find it hard to appreciate why it is so difficult for Christians to abandon a missionary approach. This approach has been dominant in Christian thinking for nearly two hundred years. Missionaries have been upheld as examples of heroic self-sacrifice. Traditionally Christians have made claims for the uniqueness of Jesus Christ as the only saviour. They have believed with scriptural warrant that it was their responsibility to share that salvation with others – 'to the Jew first and also to the Gentile' (Rom. 1.17). Jesus' parting words to his disciples were, according to Matthew's Gospel, 'Go forth therefore and make all nations my disciples, baptize men everywhere in the name of the Father and the Son and the Holy Spirit' (28.19) or, according to the Acts of the Apostles, 'You will bear witness for me in Jerusalem, and all over Judaea and Samaria, and away to the ends of the earth' (1.8). Both formulations, especially the Matthaean verses with their trinitarian reference, clearly do not go back to Jesus himself. Yet those most committed to mission are unlikely to adopt a critical approach to scripture. For some 'fundamentalist' Christians, the conversion of the Jews will herald the Second Coming of Christ.

Because the responsibility for mission is so deeply rooted amongst many Christians, Jews sometimes expect a more rapid change of attitude than is possible. It is unrealistic to expect the churches just to abandon the call to mission, as one draft of the 1988 Lambeth Conference document on the 'Way of Dialogue' seemed to suggest was possible.[11]

When in late 1985 and early 1986, because of the publicity given to campaigns by 'Jews for Jesus', especially on university campuses, the issue threatened to endanger the growth of dialogue, the Council of Christians and Jews issued a statement, with the approval of major church leaders. It affirmed that 'true dialogue involves mutual respect and precludes any attempt to entice or pressurize the partner to convert from one religion to the other'. It deplored any form of deception in evangelization and targetting of Jews for special missionary activity, although it recognized that groups actively engaged in evangelism were not under the control of the main churches. The statement went on: 'Throughout the centuries Christians have understood the concept of witness in various ways. Many Christians today believe that it is important to develop an understanding of witness or mission which takes into account our present recognition of God's activity among other religious faiths, and of the special relationship between Christianity and Judaism.'[12]

Reinterpretation

One way to develop such an understanding of mission is to reinterpret what is meant by mission. Dr Runcie in his Younghusband Lecture said, 'Whilst in the past the goal of Christian mission has mainly been the awakening of faith, the founding of churches, the growth and maintenance of Christian life, we now perceive more clearly . . . another goal as that of giving witness to the spirit of love and hope, of promoting justice and peace, sharing responsibility with others for the development of a caring society, especially where people are in need . . . This will mean some claims about the exclusiveness of the church have to be renounced, but also that past and present prejudices about other religions have to be overcome, and ignorance and contempt actively resisted.'[13] Sometimes there is talk of a shared mission of those who believe in God to a secularist world.

Others distinguish between mission or 'proselytism' and

'witness'. Proselytism or mission are used in a pejorative sense of the organized attempt to win members of one faith over to another and to get them to change their religion. This may not be aggressive or deceptive. It may include medical care, education and the offer of friendship. The suspicion is that none of this is disinterested if the long-term aim or hope is conversion. By contrast, it is stressed that dialogue must not have any ulterior purpose.

Witness, by contrast, is used of a telling of what the Christian believes God has done in Jesus Christ. It is a sharing of experience. No attempt is made to pressurize the other, and it is stressed that the response is a matter between the individual and God. Lord Coggan, at one time Chairman of CCJ, talked about the biblical meaning of 'conversion', 'evangelism' and 'mission'. 'The tragedy takes place when mission or evangelism is interpreted in terms of *proselytization*. That last word speaks of pressure, if not of force, of (at least would-be) compulsion – "Believe this, or else!" There is a hemisphere of difference between obedience to mission and proselytism. "The open-to-all Christ does not override the wills that do not seek. The Gospel is not coercive" (Kenneth Cragg).'[14] Lord Coggan goes on to suggest that the word *invitation* may be appropriate. Philip's reply to Nathanael, 'Come and see', 'is the essence of Christian invitation'.[15] In dialogue, the sharing of religious experience and understanding is proper, if a deep enough relationship exists (although some are hesitant about 'theological dialogue'). Rabbi Rodney Mariner says that 'in Jewish understanding the process of mission was in the main a static one; or *lagoyim* – "a light to the nations" – was more a beacon towards which those in search of a particular truth made their way than Diogenes carrying his lamp'.[16]

To what extent does this witness carry with it the hope (and prayer) that the other's belief will be changed?' There are Christians fully committed to dialogue and who reject 'proselytism', whose hope or eschatological expectation is that eventually all people will come to believe in Christ.

My own hope would be more modest, as I believe there is God-given value in the great religious traditions of the world. My hope is that the bitterness between them will disappear and that they will recognize their insights as convergent or complementary. Religions do not say the same thing, but their particular insights may illumine the divine mystery who transcends our understanding. My hope is that others can appreciate the meaning and value that Jesus Christ embodies for me, but this may be by appropriating the value they come to see in him rather than by becoming Christians. Already this is beginning to happen as some members of other faiths respond to Jesus, just as my Christian faith is enriched as I appropriate what I learn from Judaism and other faiths.[17] It is the way of 'passing over' of which John Dunne speaks.[18]

Such a view depends on the recognition of God's presence in all religious traditions. Such a view is not too difficult for Jews, as Judaism has never claimed a monopoly of truth.[19] It is a view, often labelled 'pluralism', which is gaining ground amongst Christians and for which I argued in the previous chapter.[20] This view also depends on recognizing the relativity of religious language. God is greater than our descriptions of him. 'What name can I give you, you, who are beyond all names?', as Gregory Nazianzen said long ago.[21]

In trusting dialogue, we as Christians gladly share our knowledge of God made known in Jesus Christ and we welcome what we can learn from others of their understanding of God. Such sharing is to our mutual enrichment and is a pilgrimage of hope, but it depends on an openness and trust that is at once destroyed by any suggestion that there is an ulterior motive for our conversation.

It is understandable to think that our path is the best, as we may make a similar claim for our country. Yet it is scarcely a claim that we can substantiate and one about which it is fruitless to argue. Proper pride in our heritage must also be tempered by real shame and penitence for the attitude and behaviour of the church to those of other faiths and most especially towards the Jews.

9

Shoah

The Shoah should perhaps have been the starting point of this book. It has cast its dark shadow over Christian–Jewish relations. Indeed, the horrors of the Holocaust are causing a profound reshaping of religious thought.[1] Alice and Roy Eckardt speak of 'FS' – in the year of the Final Solution. 'Fresh dating procedures serve the function of recognizing and symbolizing the watersheds of human history.'[2] It was, they say, 'a truly transcending or metahistorical event, an event that twists our journey through space-time by 180 degrees'.[3]

Yet although the Shoah was in part the result of false teaching by Christians about the Jews and Judaism, the teaching was false *per se*. There are those who suggest that Christian teaching is being changed so as 'to be nice to the Jews'. It is being changed because it was wrong. The Shoah showed the terrible effects of such wrong teaching.

Christians cannot fully enter into the sufferings of the Jewish people, but without a 'wounding sense of the Holocaust',[4] they cannot come close to them. There are many books and films, but even so it is impossible to feel the horror of the atrocities and to plumb the depth of human cruelty. The Orthodox Jewish thinker, Eliezer Berkovits, writes: 'However much, and however deeply, those who were not there may identify with the sufferings of the victims, their experience remains forever merely a vicarious shadow of the actual event, as removed from the reality of the holocaust as is the rather comfortable scholarship of the radical theologians of our day from the universe of the concentration camps and the crematoria.'[5]

'Most people in our time,' says the Israeli poet Yehuda Amichai, 'have the face of Lot's wife: turned towards the Holocaust, yet always escaping.'[6] Many perhaps scarcely have their face turned towards these events, as a younger generation grows up ignorant of recent history. Others tend to generalize the word, so the particular horror of the Nazi attack on the Jews is clouded over.

The uniqueness of the Holocaust

The term 'holocaust' is theological in origin rather than historical. It is an English derivative from the Greek translation of the Hebrew *olah*, which means a sacrificial offering burnt whole before the Lord. Some think the word already softens the horror by importing a religious meaning. The Hebrew (and so also Yiddish) word 'Churban', meaning 'destruction', is more stark and refers to the results of the event itself. The word, however, is found in rabbinic literature and is used to describe the destruction of the first and second Temples. Using it of the Shoah may imply some connection between these three traumas in Jewish history. The Hebrew 'Shoah' ('destruction') is free from both historical and theological associations.

It is not always clear whether those who speak of the Holocaust are referring to the destruction of six million Jews by the Nazis or to the Nazis' systematic murder of eleven million people, of whom six million were Jews and others were gypsies, homosexuals, the mentally ill, and opponents of the Third Reich.

The survivor and poet Elie Wiesel stresses that the word should be confined to the six million Jews, as the attack on them was *sui generis*. 'Not all the victims were Jews, but all Jews were victims.'[7] Simon Wiesenthal, however, argues that by referring to eleven million you broaden support for their remembrance. Michael Berenbaum of George Washington University says that in his opinion, 'the task of the USA Holocaust Memorial Council involves the Americanization of the Holocaust: that is, the story must be told in such a way that it resonates not only with the survivor in New York, his son in Houston or his daughter in San Francisco, but with the Black leader from Atlanta and his child, the farmer from the Midwest, the industrialist from the Northeast, and the millions of other Americans who each year make a pilgrimage to Washington to visit their nation's capital.'[8]

This allows the Holocaust to symbolize man's inhumanity to man and to include the genocide of the Armenians, the victims of Idi Amin in Uganda, those massacred on the killing fields of South East

Asia, and many others who have suffered violent and untimely deaths. Yet this submerges the specific Jewish tragedy and may allow us to evade facing latent antisemitism. Many are disgusted by the fact that at Babi Yar, the Russian memorial does not mention that the victims of the massacre were Jewish, either in the context of the sculpture or in the memorial inscription. One reason for the objections to the Carmelite Convent at Auschwitz was that in a similar way it obscured the specifically Jewish tragedy and this reflected the usual attitude of the Polish authorities.

During the war, the allies were reluctant to highlight the atrocities, as they did not want to appear to be fighting to 'rescue the Jews'. There are those too today, such as revisionists, who find the easiest way to remove blame from Hitler is to lament the 'terrible things done in war', and to put the Holocaust in a catalogue that includes the bombing of Dresden and of Hiroshima. All unnecessary and cruel death is to be deplored, but easily we evade the specific nature of the Nazi attack on the Jews, as Jews. There was no way out. A person could not renounce her Jewishness, even if for a couple of generations she had been a Christian. (Most Jews feel Edith Stein died for her Jewishness rather than as a Christian martyr.) A Jew could not submit to the political views of his persecutors. Jews were doomed to destruction for their very Jewishness – by birth, not because of actions or beliefs. Even Himmler said, 'Every German knows one good Jew', but character, like age and sex, was irrelevant in the democracy of the gas chambers.

The Nazi attack was also systematic, whereas the pogroms of earlier periods were the outbursts of mob fury, albeit sometimes abetted by the authorities. Pogroms were not carefully planned, whereas the Final Solution was carried out with clinical detachment. Trains needed to move troops to the front were diverted to transport Jews to the death camps. To save the cost of a pennyworth of gas, children were thrown alive into the crematoria's fires. Bodies were treated as expendable raw material; gold stoppings were removed from the teeth, hair was shaved off to stuff mattresses, and the ashes were used in fertilizers – not to mention the use of living bodies for medical experiments. These were not the exigencies of the battlefield, but the decisions of distant bureaucrats (reminding us of the terrifying anonymity, remoteness and impersonality of modern war).

Earlier attacks on the Jews were episodic and not sustained. They were often illegal and they were based on religious bigotry. The Nazi attacks were unrelenting expressions of their racial discrimination.[9]

The Nazi attempt to destroy European Jewry can indeed be compared to other acts of genocide, such as the Turkish massacre of the Armenians, but its specific character needs also to be remembered, lest we evade the antisemitism and anti-Judaism of Western and Christian culture.

Christian responsibility for anti-Judaism

It was within Christendom that the Holocaust occurred. 'The Holocaust did not mark the end of the Jewish people . . . The Holocaust for its utter bestiality, tolled the knell of Europe and Christendom, who tolerated it, and whose culture produced it. It is said that the Nazis carried out in detail the treatment that Luther had ordained with regard to the Jews, which was also in line with Catholic tradition.'[10]

This quotation is from a Jewish newsletter, dated March 1986. It reflects a viewpoint, widespread amongst Jews, that the Holocaust happened in a Christian country. Christians, of course, today, would totally disown Hitler, even though he had some supporters in the churches at the time. Yet it depends on what is meant by a 'Christian country'. Committed Christians are very aware that twentieth-century Europe is not, in a real sense, 'Christian'. People in other parts of the world, however, regard it as such, just as Europeans think of Iran or Saudi Arabia as 'Muslim' countries. Again, it is not enough to point to those Christians, 'the righteous Gentiles', who opposed Hitler, often at great cost. Nor is it sufficient to say that the Allies fought against Nazism. Whilst Hitler was an aberration, it was in a country shaped for centuries by Christian culture, a country noted for its intellectual and artistic achievements, that this virulent antisemitism erupted.[11]

Martin Gilbert begins his massive study of the Holocaust with these words: 'For many centuries, primitive Christian Europe had regarded the Jew as the "Christ killer", an enemy and a threat, to be converted and so be "saved", or to be killed, to be expelled, or to be put to death with sword and fire.'[12] The age-long anti-Judaism of the churches prepared the seed-ground on which the vicious weed of Nazism could grow so rapidly. This has to be acknowledged honestly by Christians, if a new healthier relationship with Jews is to grow. It has also to be acknowledged for the health of Christianity itself. For the exclusivist attitude to the Jews is related to male domination in the churches and to racism and attitudes of superiority towards other peoples and cultures.[13]

There are questions of immediate responsibility, such as whether the churches could have done more to oppose Hitler. In Martin Niemoller's famous words:

> First they came for the socialists, and I did not speak out – because I was not a socialist.
> Then they came for the trade unionists, and I did not speak out – because I was not a trade unionist.
> Then they came for the Jews, and I did not speak out – because I was not a Jew.
> Then they came for me – and there was no one left to speak for me.[14]

The role of Pope Pius XII has been much debated and questions have been asked about why Hitler was not excommunicated.[15] There have been questions, too, about why the Allies did not bomb the railway approaches to Auschwitz.

These are now questions of historical research and debate, although our reading of history continues to colour the present. The urgent need is for the churches to purge themselves of all anti-Jewish teaching. Many of the issues have been discussed elsewhere, but it is worth bringing them together here in summary form.

The traditional view was that the Jews rejected their Messiah and crucified him. God, therefore, punished the Jews, by destroying Jerusalem and scattering them in exile. The Jews had forfeited the promises made to them in the *old* Covenant and these promises had been taken over by the church, the *new* Israel, which lived by grace not law.[16] Often Christians came to speak of the Jews as 'children of the devil', invented infamous libels about them, made them wear distinctive dress and forced them to live in ghettos.[17]

Different aspects of this outline were emphasized at different times, but Christians now increasingly recognize that it is a tissue of lies. Jesus was not the Messiah of Jewish expectation. It was not 'the Jews' who crucified him. God did not abandon his covenant with Israel. Rather, it is one God of mercy and justice who speaks through the whole Bible. The Old Testament is not a 'religion of law', and in the New Testament, the Pharisees are caricatured. Jesus seems to have been close to them in his teaching. The decisive and bitter parting of the ways between those who believed in Jesus and those who did not took place after the fall of Jerusalem. Two creative religious traditions emerged from common roots in the Hebrew Bible: Rabbinical Judaism and the early church, which was soon predominantly Gentile.

Gradually Christians, aware of the horrors of the Holocaust and of the church's share of responsibility, are revising their teaching and accepting this new picture. Slowly they are starting to grapple with the theological implications of this revision. There are, however, also profound questions about our understanding of human nature and our belief in God which are questions not just to Christians, but to all believers. Questions which some Jews and Christians are starting to ponder together.

Is forgiveness possible?

The fortieth anniversary of the Allied victory in Europe brought vivid reminders of the horrors of the Holocaust. For that victory was accompanied by the opening of the concentration camps. It also brought to the fore questions about how we today relate to those events – questions highlighted by President Reagan's visit to the cemetery at Bitsburg, where amongst others, some members of the SS were buried.

The temptation is to forget. The Jews feel that on the whole the world would rather not know. There are so-called 'revisionists' who suggest that the Holocaust never happened or was greatly exaggerated. For example, the Institute for Historical Review 1979 Revisionist Convention, which met in Los Angeles, resolved that 'the allegations that gas chambers existed in occupied Europe during World War II are demonstrably false'.[18] Others seek to 'whitewash' Hitler, perhaps by suggesting that he was ignorant of what happened. Others seek to generalize the Holocaust – and the word now tends to be used to describe almost any disaster – by seeing it as one amongst many of the horrific events of war.

Others perhaps just feel that it was a long time ago and wonder what good it does to harp on the past. One has now to be middle-aged to have been alive when Hitler was in power. This, however, evades facing the horror and for Christians can be a way of evading responsibility. If Christians suggest the time has come 'to forgive and forget', it may be that it is Christians who cannot bear to face their guilty past. 'We made up the world in which the Holocaust happened,' wrote Alan Ecclestone, an Anglican scholar and parish priest, in his moving book *The Night Sky of the Lord*.[19] Unless this responsibility is acknowledged, Christians will not come close to their Jewish brothers and sisters.

Christians need also to try to enter into Jewish insecurity. I recall watching a film about the son of a survivor. As he relived his father's experiences, he sensed the same antisemitism all around him in New York and had the nightmare of a new holocaust happening there. Eventually he emigrated (*aliyah*) to Israel. For many Jews, Israel is their only security. The rest of the world was unable or unwilling to protect Jewry from the wrath of Hitler. Would it protect Jews today from a new onslaught of antisemitism?

But does remembering, like scratching a spot, mean that the wound continues to fester, not only reinforcing the bitterness and hostility many Jews feel, but itself renewing antagonism? This was the concern voiced by Canon Dr Anthony Phillips, at the time Chaplain of St John's College, Oxford, and Consultant to the Archbishop on Jewish affairs, in an article in *The Times* in the summer of 1985. It was given the heading 'Why the Jews must forgive'. The thought that Christians were giving the Jews a lecture on morality was much resented. The final sentence of the article was also resented. It could be read as implying that the Jews in some sense invited their own sufferings. 'In remembering the Holocaust,' Dr Phillips wrote, 'Jews hope to prevent its recurrence: by declining to forgive, I fear they unwittingly invite it.'[20] His concern was that bitterness and evil which are not forgiven fester and breed new bitterness, as in Northern Ireland. 'To forgive and forget is naive, as President Reagan's original proposal to visit Bitsburg but not Belsen was naive. But to remember and not to forgive can only invite further bloodshed, as the history of Ulster confirms. A theology unwilling to come to terms with the oppressors, however heinous their crimes, imprisons itself in its own past, jeopardizing the very future it would ensure. Without forgiveness there can be no healing within the community, no wholeness. The leopard cannot lie down with the kid. Indeed the opposite occurs. For failure to forgive is not a neutral act: it adds to the sum total of evil in the world and dehumanizes the victims in a way the oppressors could never on their own achieve.'[21]

In the correspondence, it became clear that Jewish and Christian concepts of forgiveness differ. In an earlier article, Rabbi Dr Albert Friedlander, of Westminster Synagogue, who has lectured widely on the Holocaust, had written that at a Kirchentag (or Church Conference) in Nuremberg, 'I talked about the anguish of Auschwitz. A young girl rushed up to me after the lecture, "Rabbi," she said, "I wasn't there, but can you forgive me?" and we embraced and cried together. Then an older man approached me. "Rabbi," he said, "I was a guard at a concentration camp. Can you forgive me?" I looked at him. "No," I said, "I cannot forgive. It is not the function of rabbis to give absolution, to be pardoners. In Judaism, there is a ten-day period of penitence, between the New Year and the Day of Atonement, when we try to go to any person whom we have wronged and ask for forgiveness. But you cannot go to the six million. They are dead and I cannot speak for them. Nor can I speak for God. But you are here at a church conference. God's forgiving grace may touch you: but I am not a mediator, pardoner, or spokesman for God."'[22]

In Jewish thought, forgiveness is a prerogative of God. Rabbis are not priests. Forgiveness also requires restitution to the injured, which was impossible to the victims. No one could pronounce forgiveness in their name. Further, forgiveness follows repentance, and Jews ask, is there evidence of this?

Some Christians would echo this, whereas others, reflecting on the parable of the prodigal son, believe that the injured party has to take the initiative if there is to be reconciliation. 'God was in Christ, reconciling the world unto himself, not imputing their trespasses unto them' (II Cor. 5.19). The wronged one, by taking the pain upon himself, absorbs the bitterness and makes healing possible.

In the ensuing discussion, the danger that hatred and anger can embitter and erode was recognized. Eugene Heimler, an Auschwitz survivor, wrote: 'If we, those of us who survived the camps, limit ourselves to grieving only over our tragedy, harbouring a continuous depression or anger, then we will not do justice to the magnitude of the tragedy and will fail even to try to turn it into a healing experience . . . Any sensible psychologist knows that to remain beyond a reasonable time in a state of depression and anger is sick and self-destructive.'[23] Albert Friedlander wrote, 'We have taught Freud enough out of the sources of Judaism to understand what damage buried resentments can do to our psyche.'[24] There was some recognition of the misuse of the Holocaust by Jews, in the words of Rabbi Bayfield, who is Director of the Sternberg Centre for Judaism, by 'manipulating it to provoke unnecessary guilt, playing it as a card to end debates and arguments, shutting off discussion by inappropriate breast beating'.[25] Sometimes, too, it seems to be used politically to gain support for Israel. Visiting statesmen seem to be taken almost at once to the Holocaust memorial, Yad Vashem. There was some resentment, however, that Christians should appear to tell Jews how to handle their grief and it was said that coping with bitterness is not the same as forgiving.

There was serious questioning whether the offer of unconditional forgiveness allows the sinner to confront what he has done and to change his ways. 'An empty formula of forgiveness represses resentment just as much as open rejection of the unrepentant sinner – and rejection gives the sinner another opportunity to change his way.'[26] There is a rabbinical saying, 'Whoever is merciful to the cruel will end by being indifferent to the innocent'.[27] Perhaps here there may be a difference between our own feelings towards one who has injured us and our concern for others who have been injured and their proper demand for justice or redress. There is an individual response, but also we contribute to the collective response to wrong-doing, which is expressed through the exercise of justice.

The key point was whether repentance is a prior necessity before forgiveness is possible. Rabbi Bayfield stresses that the Jewish God is a forgiving God, 'as the climactic phrase in the Yom Kippur (Day of Atonement) service echoes in the memory – *salachti kidvarecha* – "I have forgiven as you ask"'.[28] But, first, 'man has to humble himself, acknowledge his wrong and resolve to depart from sin'.[29] 'Forgiveness is always and only consequent on repentance.'[30] Maimonides taught that if a person has injured his neighbour, 'he will never find forgiveness until he has rendered back to his neighbour what he owes him and has begged forgiveness of him'.[31] 'The central requirement of the Jewish tradition,' writes Rabbi Bayfield, 'is repentance.'[32] Dr Friedlander says the same: 'The stress is clear: the winning of forgiveness depends upon the actions of the sinner; the wrong done must be acknowledged and confessed; it must have become abhorrent to the sinner. The sinner must change before receiving forgiveness, and public acts of fasting and self-abasement must be followed by actions demonstrating a change of heart and a new way of life.'[33]

This is where some Christians would differ and suggest that the initiative for reconciliation may have to lie with the one injured. Anthony Phillips quotes an Editorial from *Common Ground*, the journal of the Council of Jews and Christians in Britain, from 1968: 'And bitter, unfair, unreasonable though it may seem to be, the healed relationship can only come through the activity of the sufferer. This is a point of anguish – something which can scarcely be said though it is necessary to say it.'[34]

There are a number of elements in such a Christian approach. Because of the doctrine of original sin, the Christian believer knows his or her affinity with the worst sinner. So although there may be great difference in people's character and behaviour, all, in Paul's words, 'have sinned and come short of the glory of God' (Rom. 3.23). All stand in need of the mercy of God. Albert Friedlander comments on this: 'Basically Judaism is opposed to original sin. Man/Woman is good. We stumble off the right path, but we can return to it. If we seriously accepted original sin, if we had to live with the fact that all humans are tainted and that they cannot remove guilt from themselves – we might well be pushed into a position more often encountered in Christianity. All have been washed clean by the blood of the lamb who have accepted the Christ – dare we set ourselves against the Lord who has forgiven them? Must we not accept our brother and sister in Christ who have been forgiven by God?'[35] Dr Friedlander answers his question with a 'No'.

Christians are also conscious of the grace of God working in them and they will be reluctant to judge others. 'There but for the grace of God go I.' It is too easy to think of the Nazis as wicked, rather than to recognize the evil within each one of us. Anthony Phillips quotes from the Jewish Michel Goldberg's book, *Namesake*, where he tells how he tracked down the Nazi criminal Klaus Barbie hiding in Bolivia. But faced with the opportunity of killing him, he turned away. He wrote: 'Actually, I had just inflicted defeat on myself. It was the first, in the area most important to me and probably the only one in which I was vulnerable. Was it to make myself tougher or to cure me? It is not Barbie I killed but myself, the person I had been up to then. So I did kill a Nazi in La Paz, but not the one I had planned to kill.'[36]

Dr Phillips stressed that the call for forgiveness arises from taking seriously the doctrine of creation. He quoted Kenneth Kirk, a former Bishop of Oxford, who wrote: 'There must be something bracing, inspiring, creative in his attitude towards them – something to make new men of them. To forgive is not merely to "overlook", or to "forget" or to "say no more about" the past; it is to inspire a new effort by an act or attitude of unexpected graciousness. Forgiveness of others, therefore, can only come from an over-whelming zeal for their spiritual welfare; if that zeal be impeded by consciousness of injury done by them, it must be roused to activity by a consideration of their infinite value in God's sight.'[37] Dr Phillips continued: 'In the desire to forgive, man aligns himself with the continual divine process of re-creation which frees him from the nightmare of the past, enabling him to draw nearer to that eschatological kingdom in which the leopard lies down with the kid. Without forgiveness there can be no peace – the world can only groan and travail, controlled by its past.'[38] The doctrine of creation also suggests that all human beings are precious to God because created in his image, however much they have defiled it.

The Christian believes, too, that no hardened sinner is beyond the possibility of redemption. 'Christ died for us whilst we were yet sinners' (Rom. 5.8). This has been confirmed for many Christians in their own conversion experience. There is repeated emphasis in Christian devotion on God in Christ seeking the one who is lost.

Amazing grace! How sweet the sound
That saved a wretch like me.
I once was lost, but now am found,
Was blind, but now I see.[39]

Further, it is in being made aware of love and acceptance that the evildoer comes to self-knowledge. To proclaim the all-forgiving love of God is not to condone evil. The forgiveness is offered freely, but its appropriation necessarily expresses itself in repentance. As Dorothy Sayers put it: 'While God does not and man dare not demand repentance as a condition for bestowing pardon, repent-ance remains an essential condition for receiving it.'[40] Zacchaeus gives half his goods to charity (Luke 19.8). 'Forgive us our trespasses, as we forgive those who trespass against us', does not mean that our forgiveness is conditional on our forgiving others, but that truly to know forgiveness is to become forgiving towards others. The point is illustrated in the parable of the generous master and the unforgiving servant (Matt. 18.23–35).

Ed Sanders suggests that this was one area where Jesus disagreed with the Pharisees. If so, the radical nature of Jesus' understanding of God's love is as disturbing to the Christian church as it was to his Jewish contemporaries. His picture of a divine love that goes on loving the worst sinner, offering to him the possibility of repentance, contrasts sharply with traditional Christian teaching about heaven and hell, with the belief that many are in agony for all eternity. The alternative picture of God implies a 'universalism' – that God's will is the salvation of all and that his salvation is not complete until all have accepted his love and in accepting it come to penitent self-knowledge.[41]

Albert Friedlander echoes much of the same compassion and hope: 'We believe and celebrate the goodness and compassion of God, his infinite capacity to forgive. We cannot arrogate his judgment to ourselves. All humans have the capacity to sin, and all have the capacity to return . . . We can have compassion for damaged, tainted human beings who have come to personify evil in the world. We can hope that they will return and repent. We can and do recommend them to the judgment and compassion of God. But, here in this world, we have also to defend standards of justice and must fight against evil.'[42]

Is the way of forgiving love strong enough to overcome the evil of the world? This is the haunting question with which all the discussion leaves me. It is not possible to say what one would do in a hypothetical situation. It is presumptuous to tell others what they should do – especially those who have been deeply scarred and injured. Wonderfully, some Jews, such as Otto Frank and Albert Friedlander himself, have given themselves to the task of reconciliation. For me belief in Jesus is commitment to his way of nonviolent, suffering, forgiving love and this is why I believe Christian pacifism to be integral to the Gospel. But this is the risk of faith, which cannot be made lightly – aware as we are of the horrors of the Holocaust and other acts of bestial cruelty in this century. There is a profound evil in human affairs. Is it possible to believe that God can restore and redeem even this, or is there an element of loss and an evil which must only be destroyed?

Because the cross and resurrection are so central to the Christian faith, there is a deep-seated Christian conviction that suffering may be redemptive. Evil is not total loss, but may be transformed. As Dr Phillips wrote, 'Suffering is always wicked, cruel and devilish, but it need not be useless and uncreative. It can have a redemptive power far beyond any human anticipation.'[43] This is not a Jewish response, where there is a recognition of sheer evil and loss. In words of Rabbi Hugo Gryn, 'You will not find in Judaism the notion which, as I understand it, is rather basic to Christianity, namely that suffering leads to salvation.'[44]

Very properly, there is a feeling that to seek some meaning in the Holocaust mitigates what happened. There is dislike, too, of the way some Christian thinkers link Auschwitz and Calvary – appearing to read Christian values into Jewish misery, a misery partly itself caused by Christians.[45] Yet, however great the sensitivity and awareness, it seems to emerge from the debate that whereas for many Christians only love counts, in Rabbi Bayfield's words, 'the Jewish image of God is subtly different. As the Talmud says, "What does the Holy One, blessed be He, pray?" Rav Zutra bar Tovi said in the name of Rav, "May it be My will that My mercy suppresses My anger and that My mercy will prevail over My other attributes, so that I may deal with My children in the attribute of mercy and, on their behalf, stop short of the limit of strict justice". That struggling, that soul searching, that balancing of justice with mercy is the Jewish paradigm.'[46] If Christians seem more confident in their declarations about the character of God, they need to listen to the Jewish questions, and perhaps they still have to come to terms with the impact of the Holocaust on all faith in God's goodness.

10

Faith after Auschwitz

The Shoah is a challenge to all belief in God. The reality of such evil needs to be grappled with by Christian theologians. From America, Harvey Cox has said that all theology today starts after the Holocaust. From Germany, Johann-Baptist Metz has put it like this:

> There is no truth for me which I could defend with my back turned toward Auschwitz.
> There is no sense for me which I could save with my back turned toward Auschwitz.
> And for me there is no God to whom I could pray with my back turned toward Auschwitz.[1]

Whilst many continental European and American theologians are grappling with Holocaust theology, its impact seems to have been far less on British theologians. This gives the impression that there is a reluctance both to take seriously enough the pervasive anti-Jewishness of Christian teaching and to face the deep questions to faith posed by the Shoah.

Reflecting on the Shoah has made me more aware of the depth of human evil and more hesitant to repeat traditional statements about God's almighty power. Christians still, popularly, speak as if God will put everything right. Yet if he 'allowed' six million of his people to be exterminated, the credibility of all statements about God's power or God's love are called in question. Indeed distorted pictures of God's power are not unrelated to the abuse of power and the degradation of minorities in European history.

Because the Holocaust is a central defining event of contemporary Jewish thought and consciousness, it is important for Christians to be aware of Jewish thinking if they are to come closer to an understanding of the Jewish world today. This awareness may at least prevent Christians from making comments on the Holocaust which are wounding or offensive to Jews and which poison Christian–Jewish relations. It may also help Christians as they ponder the deep questions to faith posed by the Shoah – questions which are a challenge to all believers.

Jewish responses

There have been various Jewish responses to the Holocaust. Many, perhaps often not the most articulate or at least not those much read outside the Orthodox Jewish world, have maintained the view, which has played a large part in traditional teaching, that suffering is mainly a punishment for sin. The cogency of such views, as Rabbi Dr Norman Solomon has perceptively pointed out, depends heavily on the belief in life after death. 'Such beliefs simplify the theology of suffering, for (*a*) they diminish the significance of the vicissitudes of "this world" and (*b*) they provide an opportunity for "compensation" for the evils of this world in the next.'[2] Traditional Jewish teaching clearly distinguishes between individual and collective providence. In terms of the latter, the destruction of part of the people of Israel can be seen as belonging to God's redemptive process, leading ultimately to Israel's restoration. To the very Orthodox also, with their high concept of the ideal demanded by Torah, Jewry was lax in its observance. Elchanan Wasserman, a disciple of the saintly Chafetz Chayim, was one of the leading rabbis of the pre-war generation. In 1938, he visited the USA and was dismayed by the lack of Torah learning and observance amongst the Jews he met. There he completed his pamphlet, *Iqvata diMechichta* (In the Footsteps of the Messiah), in which he predicted that dire destruction would come upon the Jewish people on account of its lack of faith and its laxity in the observance of God's commandments.

To some, also, the harshness of God's punishment was a sign of his special love. In Wasserman's pamphlet also there is a sense of apocalyptic, of being part of the events heralding the Messiah and the final redemption of Israel and the world (comparable to the beliefs of some fundamentalist Christians that the return to Israel is in preparation for the Second Coming). This is linked to ideas of atonement and sacrifice. Rabbi Israel Shapiro of Grodinsk, together with his Hasidim, were herded into box cars and transported from Warsaw to Treblinka. When they arrived, he told his Hasidim that these were at last the real birth-pangs of the Messiah, and that he and they were blessed, for their ashes would help purify Israel and thus hasten the end.[3]

Other Jewish writers, however, feel traditional teaching is no longer adequate after the Shoah, although Dr Solomon suggests the inadequacy has nothing to do with the Shoah, because the answers never were satisfactory.[4]

One response is to deny God and hope. This may be the unvoiced view of a number of Jews, but it has been eloquently expressed by the philosopher Richard Rubenstein. He tells of the effect on him of an interview with Dean Grüber, who held that the Nazi slaughter of Jews was somehow God's will. 'After my interview I reached a theological point of no return – If I believed in God as the omnipotent author of the historical drama and Israel as His Chosen People, I had to accept Dean Grüber's conclusion that it was God's will that Hitler committed six million Jews to slaughter. I could not possibly believe in such a God nor could I believe in Israel as the chosen people of God after Auschwitz.'[5] 'We learned in the crisis that we were totally and nakedly alone, that we could expect neither support nor succour from God nor from our fellow creatures. Therefore the world will forever remain a place of pain, suffering, alienation and ultimate defeat.'[6]

The Nobel Prize winner Elie Wiesel also eloquently voiced the shattering impact of the terror.

> Never shall I forget the little faces of the children, whose bodies I saw turned into wreaths of smoke beneath a silent blue sky.
> Never shall I forget those flames which consumed my faith forever.
> Never shall I forget that nocturnal silence which deprived me, for all eternity, of the desire to live.
> Never shall I forget those moments which murdered my God and my soul and turned my dreams to dust.
> Never shall I forget these things, even if I am condemned to live as long as God Himself. Never.[7]

Some see testimony to the Lord of history in the birth of Israel. There are those for whom Israel has really become a religious substitute. The Holocaust and the creation of Israel have been compared by some Jewish writers to the death and resurrection of Jesus – with the interval of three years, instead of three days. The unparalleled destruction is followed by the unparalleled recreation of the state after two thousand years. 'Israel,' writes Rabbi Dr E. Fackenheim, a leading Jewish philosopher, 'is collectively what every survivor is individually – a "no" to the demons of Auschwitz, a "yes" to Jewish survival and security and thus a testimony to life against death, on behalf of all mankind.'[8] He stresses the duty of Jews to survive, so as not to grant a posthumous victory to Hitler.[9] 'For the sake of Jewish survival,' he writes, 'we are forbidden . . . to deny or despair of God however much we may have to contend with him or with belief in him, lest Judaism perish.'[10]

Professor Irving Greenberg, who has written particularly about the ethical impact of the Holocaust, also speaks of Israel. 'Israel's faith in the God of History demands that an unprecedented event of destruction be matched by an unprecedented act of redemption, and this has happened.'[11] He speaks also of the breakdown of the secular Absolute. Rationalism, he claims, allowed for totalitarian mass movements and the surrender of moral judgment. Only a standard of moral absolutes is strong enough to resist such evil. He also affirms life after death. 'The moral necessity of a world to come, and even of resurrection, arises powerfully out of encounter with the Holocaust.'[12]

Others see Job as a model, whose suffering is not justified by God but with whom, out of the whirlwind, God restores contact. The sense of the Presence gives the strength to go on living in the contradictions. 'We must believe in God,' Berkovits says, 'because Job believed.'[13] Martin Buber spoke of 'moment gods', that faith and unfaith are continually struggling with each other. 'We have to speak of "moment faiths", when the redeemer and the vision of redemption are present, interspersed with times when the flames and smoke of the burning children blot out faith – though it flickers again.'[14] There is not a simple division between faith and unfaith, between believer and atheist, but rather there is this struggle in everyone. 'The difference between the sceptic and the believer is the frequency of faith and not the certitude of position . . . Neither Exodus nor Easter wins out or is totally blotted out by Buchenwald, but we encounter both polar experiences. The life of faith is lived between them.'[15]

Rabbi Arthur J. Lelyveld is prepared to raise questions about divine omnipotence. He says that we have no choice but to recognize that gargantuan evil exists and is uncontrolled by God. 'We cannot pretend to know why – we can only cling stubbornly to the conviction that there is meaning – *lam'rot hakol*, in spite of everything.'[16] He distinguishes the Christian God as a God who gives, whereas the Jewish God demands. The covenant obligation that is central in Judaism calls upon the Jew to be co-worker in perfecting the world. 'The greater the evil, the more insistent and the more intense, even to the point of anguish, is the demand.' However terrible the evil of the Final Solution, Rabbi Lelyveld does not find it uniquely evil. It was 'a new phenomenon only in a quantitative and technological sense'. In demanding that Jews and humankind in general confront this evil, God, Lelyveld says, sympathizes. 'In this sense, while I cannot say that God "willed" Auschwitz, I can say that God "wept" over Auschwitz.' God suffers in anguish and this divine sympathy 'enables man to enter into "partnership" with God'. Whilst he regards the suggestion that God willed the destruction as 'blasphemous', Lelyveld insists that we cannot withdraw from the sufferers 'the dignity that lies in recognition that there existed among them a willingness to die in fulfilment of a distinctive role . . . We have said that Hitler's victims were offered no alternative. This is not wholly so. They had the alternative of dying as cravens, of cursing God and their identity. All the evidence says that in overwhelming numbers they died with dignity.' Lelyveld believes we can affirm that there is meaning and purpose in the whole and that there is cosmic evolution 'toward greater love, greater harmony and greater justice . . . When God is the guarantor of value and the source of demand, then the confrontation of evil elicits not the plaintive "Why did God do this?" but rather "What does God ask of me?".'[17]

Eliezer Berkovits also recognizes divine culpability for evil and suffering, but also does not deny God. Human freedom does not excuse God. 'God is responsible for having created a world in which man is free to make history.'[18] 'God's dominion over the world is not a dominion of justice. In terms of justice he is guilty. He is guilty of creation.' Yet, Berkovits maintains, it is still possible to trust in God, in a dimension beyond but fulfilling history, in which the tragedy of humankind will find a transformation. 'It is perhaps what God desires – a people, to whom he owes so much, who yet acknowledges Him: children, who have every reason to condemn His creation, yet accept the creator in the faith that in the fullness of time the divine indebtedness will be redeemed and the divine adventure with man will be approved even by its martyred victims.' The covenant no longer has the character of demand or even request. As Irving Greenberg has suggested, the covenant is resurrected as a wholly voluntary readiness on the part of the Jews to continue to bear the yoke of Torah.

Rabbi Ignaz Maybaum, one of the leading post-war theologians of Anglo-Jewry, who died in 1976, developed the idea of the atoning suffering of the Jewish people – dying for the sins of humankind. Their suffering was to advance God's rule over the world, awakening the conscience of the nations. 'Their deaths purged Western civilization so that it can again become a place where man can live, do justly, love mercy and walk humbly with God.'[19] Maybaum says that the planned genocide did not succeed and that God saved a remnant, as a perennial witness to his presence in the world and in the historical process.

Many Jews have lost faith in God, but others retain the hope that the future will reveal that all the suffering of the camps was not totally in vain. It may contribute to the redemption of the world by human repentance and change. The understanding of God, however, is different. A picture emerges of a God who longs for that change and weeps over human suffering, but who has no power to impose his will on human history.

Christian responses

Amongst Christian writers, perhaps the most important development has been the tendency to reinterpret the traditional doctrine of the impassibility of God to suggest that God shares the pain of those who suffer. Christian writers, however, have not avoided the danger of appearing to take over or 'Christianize' the suffering of the Jews. The distinguished German theologian Jürgen Moltmann has written, 'To recognize God in the crucified Christ means to grasp the trinitarian history of God and to understand oneself and this whole world with Auschwitz and Vietnam, with race hatred and hunger, as existing in the history of God. God is not dead. Death is in God. God suffers by us. He suffers with us. Suffering is in God.'[20] Elsewhere he writes, 'It is necessary to remember the martyrs, so as not to become abstract. Of them and of dumb sacrifices, it is true in a real, transferred sense, that God himself hung on the gallows as Elie Wiesel was able to say. If that is taken seriously, it must also be said that like the cross of Christ, even Auschwitz is in God Himself. Even Auschwitz is taken up into the grief of the Father, the surrender of the Son and the power of the Spirit.'[21]

Interpreting so Jewish a tragedy in Christian terms may, however, cause misunderstanding. As Dr Albert Friedlander has written: 'When it (Christianity) presses Judaism into its own construct, denying Judaism integrity and identity, and when it utilizes and misuses Auschwitz in a celebration of Christian triumphalism and supersessionism, we take issue with Christianity.'[22] An example of this misuse is a sentence by the Catholic theologian Clemens Thoma, which is quoted approvingly by Franz Mussner: 'For a believing Christian, the sense of the sacrificial way walked by the Jews under the Nazis . . . *is not too difficult to determine.*' He continues: 'The approximately six million Jews killed in Auschwitz and elsewhere lead his [the Christian's] thoughts first of all to Christ, with whom these Jewish masses have become one in suffering and death. Auschwitz *is the most eminent modern* sign of the inmost relationship and oneness of the Jewish martyrs . . . with the crucified Christ, although the Jews affected here could not have been aware of this. The Holocaust is thus, for the believing Christian, an *important* sign of the unbreakable unity, founded upon Christ crucified, of Judaism and Christianity in spite of *all breaks, separate ways and misunderstandings.*'[23] Another example is these words of Franz Mussner: 'Confronting the "total sacrifice" of the Jews in Auschwitz, the Christian must openly confess his participatory guilt with antisemitism; but he cannot understand the meaning of this sacrifice without the crucified Christ, who received the sacrifice of Auschwitz within his glorified body of the cross.'[24]

By his trinitarian understanding Moltmann also seems to avoid the full challenge to traditional belief about God's power and his love. For whilst he points to God's identification with suffering, he also maintains God's freedom.[25]

The Catholic theologian Gregory Baum, however, argues that traditional understandings of the divine providence, omniscience and omnipotence must be rejected. 'God is not provident . . . in the sense that as ruler of the world he has a master plan for human history by which he provides help for the people in need, especially those who ask him for it, and by which he guides the lives of men, even while acknowledging their freedom . . . (or) in which God permitted evil and . . . calculated its damaging effects and compensated for them in the final outcome. . . . (Rather) God is provident in the sense that in whatever trap a man falls, a summons continues to address him and offer him new life that makes him more truly human.'[26] God is only omniscient in the sense that there is no situation 'in which a summons to greater insight is not available'; omnipotent only in the sense that no earthly power is stronger 'than the divine grace that frees him to wrestle with it in some way and to become more human in the process'. God does not rule from above or externally, but only from within, as 'a summons and vitality in people's lives'. Baum, therefore, affirms God's total opposition to evil. Evil is not permitted by him. 'God overcomes evil. God is constantly at work among men, summoning them and gracing them to discern the evil in human life, to wrestle against it, to be converted away from it, to correct their environment, to redirect history, to transform the human community. The death that destroys is never the will of God. On the contrary, God is the never-ending summons to life.'

The challenge is to explore God's power as the power of love, recognizing the limitations that this imposes. Some writers suggest that the freedom God gives to the universe means that the outcome itself is in the balance. These ideas were developed by some writers after the First World War who had been deeply affected by the slaughter in the trenches, such as Studdert-Kennedy, known as Woodbine Willie, or the philosopher C. E. Rolt. The latter wrote: 'God, by the very nature of His omnipotence, is bound and tied hand and foot in the midst of this evil world, and is obliged to bear, not only the physical sufferings of the whole creation, but also the far more bitter pain of human motive and sin.'[27]

W. H. Vanstone

Recently these issues have been raised again by Canon William Vanstone, an Anglican theologian and parish priest, who begins with a discussion of the phenomenology of love. He looks at behaviour which shows love to be inauthentic. Its falsity is shown first when any limit is set by the will of him who professes to love; secondly, by any attempt to control the one loved; and thirdly, by detachment. 'The lover gives to the object of his love a certain power over himself.'[28]

From the three ways in which the falsity of love is expressed, Vanstone determines three characteristics of authentic love as 'limitless, precarious and as vulnerable' (p. 51). He then reflects upon the love of God in the light of this description of authentic love. The activity of God in creation is limitless creativity. 'There are no unexpended reserves of divine power or potentiality' (p. 59), and it is seriously misleading when popular devotion suggests that God has a reserve of power with which he can intervene and overrule. The activity of God in creation is also precarious. Its outcome is not predetermined, nor its triumph foreknown. Every step contains the potential for disaster and in the tragedy at Aberfan in Wales which he cites, when a waste tip fell on a school, killing many children, 'something went wrong'. Faith believes, however, that God will not rest until the evil is redeemed. Vanstone rejects popular ideas of God's foreknowledge. 'If the purpose of God in creation is foreknown and foreordained to fulfilment, then the creation itself is vanity. Within it nothing decisive happens and nothing new, it is merely the unwinding and display of a film already made. On the other hand to interpret the creation as the work of love is to interpret it as the new, as the coming-to-be of the hitherto unknown' (p. 66).

Thirdly, Vanstone insists, the activity of God in creation must be vulnerable. This means that the issue of his love in tragedy or triumph depends upon his creation. 'The cross of Christ discloses to us the poignancy of the creation itself – the tragic possibility that, when all is given in love, all may be given in vain' (p. 70). 'The conventional representation of God,' Vanstone summarizes his argument, 'is of one by whom, in creation, nothing is expended and nothing jeopardized. Who presides serene over the assured unfolding of a predetermined purpose, whose triumph is assured before the activity begins, and who, in the appearance of giving is ever maintaining, intact and unimpaired, His own supremacy. We see in this representation more of benevolence, of condescension, of manipulation and even of possessiveness than of authentic love' (p. 74). The reality is that God genuinely does not know the outcome of the creative process. He waits upon the response of his creation. He has no reserve powers – only in unfailing self-giving love he ever seeks to redeem the tragic. Vanstone therefore recognizes the real freedom of the created universe where total freedom is the necessary consequence of God's love. The issue may be tragedy as well as triumph. God's only power is that of self-giving authentic love. This cannot prevent the horrors of history, whether caused by natural disaster or human cruelty. Yet it ever seeks to redeem and restore. Of the Aberfan disaster, Vanstone writes: 'Our faith is in a creator who does not abandon even this, nor those who suffered, wept and died in it, but He so gives Himself that He finds, for the redeeming of this, yet more to give, and knows no respite until the slag-heap has become a fair hillside, and the hearts of the parents have been enlarged by sorrow, and the children themselves understand and are glad to have so feared and wept and died' (p. 65). It is a beautiful picture and Vanstone does not minimize the reality and cruelty of evil, but it is hard to think of victims of Aberfan being so reconciled, let alone the victims of the Holocaust. Yet unless we dream of some such possibility, we have to come to terms with the defeat of love and a limitation to what is redeemable.

Hans Jonas

It is interesting to compare Vanstone's writing with a lecture first given as the Harvard University Ingersoll Lecture by the Jewish Professor Hans Jonas on 'The Concept of God After Auschwitz'. He begins with a myth. 'In the beginning, for unknowable reasons, the ground of being, or the divine, chose to give itself over to the chance and risk and endless variety of becoming. And wholly so: entering into the adventure of space and time, the deity held back nothing of itself: no uncommitted or unimpaired part remained to direct, correct, and ultimately guarantee the devious working-out of its destiny in creation. On this unconditional immanence the modern temper insists. It is its courage or despair, in any case its bitter honesty, to take our being-in-the-world seriously: to view the world as left to itself, its laws as brooking no interference, and the rigour of our belonging to it as not softened by extramundane providence. The same our myth postulates for God's being in the world . . . In order that the world might be, and be for itself, God renounced His own being, divesting Himself of His deity – to receive it back from the Odyssey of time weighted with the chance harvest of unforseeable temporal experience; transfigured or possibly even disfigured by it. In such self-forfeiture of divine integrity for the sake of unprejudiced becoming, no other fore-knowledge can be admitted than that of possibilities which cosmic being offers in its own terms: to these, God committed His cause in effacing Himself for the world.'[29] He elaborates the myth by describing the emergence of life, which leads eventually to the appearance of man. 'The advent of man means the advent of knowledge and freedom and with this supremely double-edged gift the innocence of the mere subject of self-fulfilling life has given way to the charge of responsibility under the disjunction of good and evil. To the promise and risk of this agency the divine cause, revealed at last, henceforth finds itself committed: and its issue trembles in the balance. The image of God . . . passes . . . into man's precarious trust, to be completed, saved, or spoiled by what he will do to himself and the world' (p. 467).

From the myth that he sketches, Hans Jonas tries to draw out a theological or conceptual translation. He speaks, he says, of a 'suffering God'. He distinguishes this from the Christian conception, by which he understands that the deity at one particular time entered into a situation of suffering. Rather, he speaks of suffering on the part of God from the *moment* of creation, and certainly from the creation of man.

His myth also speaks of a *becoming* God. God is affected and made different by what happens in the world. 'The Eternal progressively becomes different through the actualisation of the world process' (p. 469).

Thirdly, God is a *caring* God – 'not remote and detached and self-contained but involved with what He cares for . . . He has left something for other agents to do and thereby made His care dependent upon them. He is therefore also an endangered God, a God who risks something' (p. 470). 'This,' Hans Jonas continues, 'is not an omnipotent God . . . we cannot uphold the time-honoured (mediaeval) doctrine of absolute unlimited divine power' (p. 470).

Hans Jonas rejects the concept of omnipotent power partly on logical and ontological grounds but mainly on theological grounds – as open to genuine religious objection. 'We can have divine omnipotence together with divine goodness only at the price of complete divine inscrutability. Seeing the existence of evil in the world, we must sacrifice intelligibility in God to the combination of the other two attributes. Only a completely unintelligible God can be said to be absolutely good and absolutely powerful, and yet tolerate the world as it is. Now which of the three attributes at stake, the conjunction of any two of which excludes the third, are truly integral to our concept of God, and which, being of lesser force, must give way to their superior claim? Surely, goodness is inalienable from the concept of God and not open to qualification. Intelligibility, related to both God's nature and man's limitation, is on the latter count indeed subject to qualification, but on no account to complete elimination. The *Deus absconditus*, the hidden God, is a profoundly un-Jewish conception. Our teaching holds that we can understand God, not completely, to be sure, but something of Him – of his will, intentions, and even nature, because He has told us. There has been revelation, we have His commandments and His law, and He has directly communicated with some. Thus, a completely hidden God is not an acceptable concept by Jewish norms. But he would have to be precisely that if together with being good, He were conceived as all-powerful. After Auschwitz, we can assert with greater force than ever before that an omnipotent deity would have to be either not good or totally unintelligible. But if God is to be intelligible in some manner and to some extent (and to this we must hold), then His goodness must be compatible with the existence of evil, and this is only if He is not all-powerful. Only then can we uphold that he is intelligible and good, and there is yet evil in the world. And since we have found the concept of omnipotence to be doubtful anyway, it is this which has to give way' (p. 471).

Hans Jonas goes further, picturing God as divesting himself of any power to interfere with the physical course of things, and responding to the impact on his being of worldly events with the mutely insistent appeal of his unfulfilled aim. Hans Jonas does not elaborate his ideas, but believes that creation from nothing holds together the oneness of the divine principle with the self-limitation which permits the existence and autonomy of the world. His myth, he says, pushes further the old Jewish idea of *tzimtzum*, the contraction of divine being, as the condition for the being of the world.

He draws certain ethical conclusions from his myth and its explanation. 'The first is the transcendent importance of our deeds, of how we live our lives. If man, as our tale has it, was created "for" the image of God, rather than "in" His image; if our lives become lives in the divine countenance – then our responsibility is not defined in mundane terms alone. Our impact on eternity is for good *and* evil' (p. 474). Secondly, 'Having given Himself whole to the becoming world, God has no more to give, it is man's now to give to Him' (p. 474).

Finally, Hans Jonas speaks of the gassed and burnt children of Auschwitz and the de-faced, de-humanized phantoms of the camps. 'Another chance is not given them and eternity has no compensation for what has been missed in time . . . I like to believe that there was weeping in the heights at the waste and despoilment of humanity . . . Should we not believe that the immense chorus of such cries that has risen up in our lifetime now hangs over our world as a dark, powerful and accusing cloud? That eternity looks down upon us with a frown, wounded itself and perturbed in its depth? And might we not even feel it? . . . But even if not their shadow, certainly the shadow of the Bomb is there to remind us that the image of God is in danger as never before . . . We literally hold in our faltering hands the future of the divine adventure and must not fail Him, even if we would fail ourselves' (p. 475).

A creative risk

The darkness of the Shoah and the terrible continuing record of human cruelty make clear to me that any picture of God having a reserve of power which he did not use is incompatible with the picture of God as a being of mercy and compassion. Not only does God give the created order, with its natural laws, real freedom, he puts the future of his creation into the hands of men and women. This means the outcome of human history is genuinely open. By our actions, we create a future of joy or sorrow. God's only power is his love, which is not coercive and which holds nothing back. We can neither blame God for injustice nor assume that God will put right our evil and mistaken actions. He has shown us the way of life, but he neither compels nor compensates for us. We have to let go traditional concepts of God's omnipotence and impassibility.

Such freedom also implies that human history is marked by real loss. It may be that evil prompts reflection, repentance and a change of behaviour. This does not, however, compensate for sorrow. In one's personal life there may be mistakes or wrong actions from which we learn. Yet it would have been better if we had never made those mistakes or done those wrong actions. I find Professor Jonas more realistic than Canon Vanstone when he says of the victims:

'another chance is not given them. Eternity has no compensation for what has been missed in time.' Otherwise, we seem to reintroduce a reserve of divine power. Yet in the character of love there is a restlessness until all has been restored. We must also beware of allowing thoughts of another world to divert us from the struggle for justice here. As Martin Buber said, 'One should live as though the next world did not exist.'

In terms of making meaning of history within the context of this world, the tragedies of the past will cease to be sheer loss only as the indescribable sufferings of the innocent prompt us to work for a more just world society. For Christians, Jesus on the cross is the prototype of all innocent victims, but we must beware of theologizing about other people's sufferings. Jesus also, as I suggested in the previous chapter, points the way to forgiving love which alone can break the cycle of violence. Further, he gives us a clue to understand God as a suffering God who comforts us in our pain. 'God consoles us as a mother does. She cannot magic away the pain (although that occasionally happens!), but she holds us on her lap, renewed, sometimes in darkness without light,' writes the German theologian Dorothee Sölle.[30] God speaks only through self-giving love, ever appealing to us to make such love our own. Faith is the confidence that such love cannot in the end be defeated and the commitment to make such self-giving love one's own. There can be no certainty that it will triumph. For faith is always risky, as risky as the creative process to which God is unreservedly committed.

11

Israel

In 1887 Arthur James Balfour was Chief Secretary for Ireland. An Irishman complained to him that his policies constituted a denial of justice for the Irish people. 'Justice?', said Balfour thoughtfully, 'There isn't enough to go round.'[1] These words could well be applied to the tragically conflicting claims of Jews and Palestinians to the land of Israel or Palestine. Chaim Weitzman, for decades the guiding spirit of the World Zionist Organization, himself spoke of 'a clash of rights'.

Israel perhaps causes more misunderstanding between Christians and Jews than anything else. Christian discussion about Israel is quickly clouded by arguments about the present political situation in Israel and the Middle East. Jews feel that the importance of Israel to them is ignored and they object to lectures on how to behave from Christians. They doubt the commitment of Christians to Israel's existence. In 1980, for example, when, at the United Nations, the Jordanian delegate referred to the notorious forgery, 'The Protocols of the Elders of Zion', which speaks of a Jewish international plot to rule the world, neither the delegate of France, West Germany, USA nor Britain protested.[2]

At the same time, Jews often hear Christian criticism of Israeli government policies as veiled antisemitism and fail to listen to what Christians are saying. It is important therefore to try to see events in perspective. This requires an attempt to appreciate the significance of Israel in Jewish self-understanding, some knowledge of the history and a realistic assessment of the present situation. Only then can one, perhaps, offer a Christian reflection.

1. The Land

It is difficult for Christians to appreciate the importance of 'the Land' for Jews. The Old Testament scholar Brevard Childs in his fairly recent *Old Testament Theology* does not treat 'the Land' as one of its themes. Yet as one rabbi said to me, 'You will never understand me, unless you understand what Israel means to me'. The importance of Israel to the British Jewish community is made clear by the space given to events there in the *Jewish Chronicle*. In the USA, the Jewish lobby, with its support for Israel, is a powerful factor in American politics. Besides the vital contemporary importance of the land for survival and security, after nearly one third of world Jewry perished in the Holocaust, there is an emotional, historical, liturgical and mystical link with the Land. As the General Assembly of the Church of Scotland acknowledged in 1984, 'We have become aware of the enduring centrality of Zion in Jewish liturgy and theology throughout the ages and of how Zion is seen as an expression of the fulfilment of Biblical prophecy, a home for the dispersed, and a spiritual centre.'[3] The General Assembly of the Presbyterian Church (USA), in a statement adopted in 1987, also recognized the 'continuity of God's promise of land along with the obligations of that promise to the people Israel'.[4]

The modern Christian mood in the West is 'internationalist', and many are uneasy with the patriotism of a past age. Peter Schneider, an Anglican who worked in Israel for some time and helped to initiate dialogue there, told the apocryphal story of a Western theologian who had been enjoying his new-found camaraderie with Rabbis, but was much disillusioned by the Six Day War. He complained to his new friends, 'We have just got over the shock of having to treat Judaism as a real religion. Indeed theologically we can now cope with that, and then almost immediately, you Jews go and spoil it all by insisting in this day and age in tying up your religion with a piece of real estate.'[5] The American Henry Siegman some years ago described a figure of the Catholic radical left in these words, which would be true of many liberal Protestants. They are 'nourished by a Christian universalism which cannot abide the earthiness of Jewish particularism. . . . They cannot abide Jews who are flesh-and-blood people, who are men and women like other men and women in all their angularities and specificities, who need to occupy physical space in a real world before they fulfill whatever loftier aspirations they may have. They are distressed by the notion that Jews should want a flesh-and-blood existence as a people in the real geography of this world.'[6]

There was a similar mood amongst some Jews in the late nineteenth century, but almost all Jews now identify emotionally with Israel. In 1885, a group of American Reform rabbis issued a statement known as the Pittsburg Platform which said: 'We recognize in the modern era of universal culture, of heart and intellect, the approaching of a realization of Israel's great messianic hope for the establishment of the kingdom of truth, justice and peace among all men. We consider ourselves no longer a nation, but a religious community, and therefore expect neither a return to Palestine nor a sacrificial worship under the sons of Aaron, nor the restoration of any laws concerning the Jewish state.'[7] Many Christians would feel at home with this position, but very few Jews would now be happy with it.[8] There is a universalism in Judaism, but also a particularism. It is the latter that Christians tend to have lost, but the reassertion of local identity in, for example, Scottish or Welsh or Basque nationalism, suggests that in a world where communications have become international, people need a more local sense of identity.

Christians, too, do not necessarily feel any special identification with Christians elsewhere. There is, I suspect, no great affinity with 'Christian' militias in Lebanon or 'Christian' para-military groups in Ireland. This perhaps reflects the position of a dominant group in society, where internal divisions and distinctions will be recognized. Jews, however, tend to feel an affinity with Jews anywhere – and indeed criticism of an action by a particular Jew is very often generalized into criticism of 'Jews'.

The covenant with Israel included the promised land. Israel was called to be a holy people and any community requires physical space. The Torah was the way of life for the whole community. As with Islam, there is, in the ideal, no demarcation between the religious and the political, the secular and the sacred, to which we have become accustomed in Western Europe. All life was to be lived in accordance with the will of God.

In the Bible, the holy community exists under various political systems – under the leadership of seers and prophets, under kings, under foreign dominance – and it even survives exile. The modern nation state is not, in theory, the only way in which the holy community can express itself – although probably the only way today, even if some thinkers suggest that the nation-state is now outmoded in our global civilization. What is required is a place in which society upholds the structures and rules laid down in scripture. A society has to some extent to be described geographically. It is helpful therefore, theologically, to talk about the Land rather than the state.

In traditional Christian thought, the destruction of Jerusalem in 70 CE and the scattering of the Jewish people was God's judgment upon Israel for its rejection of his Son, Jesus Christ. Yet although the Jewish people were dispersed, the link with the Land never ceased. Three times a day, in prayer, for the past two thousand years, faithful Jews have remembered Zion, yearning to return to the land of the patriarchs and the divine promise. Each year, the Passover Seder concludes with the words, 'Next year, in Jerusalem'.

Through the centuries, a small community has lived in the Land. Before 1880, the Jewish population in Palestine was less than 25,000 people. Two-thirds of these lived in Jerusalem, where through the centuries there has been an almost unbroken Jewish presence.[9] Jewish burial rites place considerable stress on Jerusalem. For millennia, pious Jews have instructed their heirs to transfer their remains to Jerusalem for burial. Many of the Jews who settled in Jerusalem did so because they wanted to die there. In the days of the Ottoman Empire, Jews arriving in Palestine would have the reason for their journey written into their passport. Often this was 'to die in Jerusalem'.

Safed (or Zefat) was another Jewish centre with a long history. It is one of the four holy cities – the others being Jerusalem, Hebron and Tiberias. In the late Middle Ages it became a centre for the study of Kabbala, the mystical interpretation of scriptures. It was there in 1577 that a Hebrew printing press was established – the first in all Asia to use movable type.

Nineteenth- and twentieth-century Zionism has various roots. It draws on the long biblical and historical link, but also relates to nineteenth-century movements for national independence and to socialism. Once Zionism is seen as a national movement, the accusation that it is racism is intolerable, especially as Jews have so often been victims of racism.

To the Arab world, however, Israel is often considered an outpost of Western imperialism. Michael Palumbo, a Palestinian author, writes in this vein: 'The founding of a Zionist state in Palestine in 1948 was not a desperate attempt to save millions of lives (from a danger that had already passed) but just one more thinly disguised example of Western exploitation of a Third World people.'[10]

The large-scale settlement of Jews in the Land subsequent to the Balfour Declaration and the creation of the state of Israel has been fraught with controversy and conflict. For Jews escaping from Europe before the Holocaust and for those survivors who settled there afterwards it was a place of refuge. Their only security lay in their own strength.[11] Having at last escaped from situations of powerlessness, where others controlled even their continuing alive, they were determined to become masters of their own destiny. The vitality of the nation and the amazing creativity of Israelis, in almost every aspect of human endeavour, has marked the rebirth of the nation with a veritable cultural renaissance.

For some, theologically, the creation of the state of Israel was a divine response to the destruction of the Shoah. Many Jews believe it is their only guarantee against a future Holocaust.[12]

Yet the Arabs too have a long association with the area. In the middle of the seventh century Palestine came under Muslim control during the great expansion of the religion of Islam. Jerusalem is the third most holy city for Muslims after Mecca and Medina. Tradition holds that Muhammad ascended to heaven on his night journey from Jerusalem. Arabs bitterly resent suggestions that the land was empty and claim that many thousands of Palestinians were driven out by Jewish colonization.[13]

2. History

The political history of the area has always been chequered and was further complicated by the Christian crusades. For four centuries, from 1517 to 1917, Syria, of which Palestine was a part, was under the sway of the Ottoman Turks. The first *aliyah*, or settlement, was a consequence of the renewed antisemitic attacks in Russia. With the accession of Alexander III (1881–1894), any hopes of gradual emancipation were shattered by a new pogrom. 'The assassination of Alexander II,' writes Conor Cruise O'Brien, the Irish diplomat, in his detailed historical study *The Siege*, 'is one of the great turning points in world history and especially in the history of the Jews'.[14] The Jews of Russia realized that antisemitism was there to stay as official government policy and that the hope of integration was a chimera. Many Russian Jews prepared to endure yet more of the age-old suffering inflicted on their people. Others decided to leave Russia. A large number left for Western Europe and the USA, where integration seemed possible. A smaller group left for Palestine, determined no longer to be settlers in an alien land. Facing great physical hardship, they started to create Jewish communities on the Land.

In Western Europe, the last decade of the nineteenth century saw Friedrich Nietzsche give intellectual respectability to antisemitism, whilst in 1894 the notorious Dreyfus affair showed the limits to liberalism in France. Dreyfus, a Jewish officer, was found guilty of treason on evidence eventually shown to be perjured. Theodor Herzl, the founder of Zionism, attended the ceremony of Dreyfus' military degradation as a journalist. Although the point is debated, Herzl himself, some four years later, said that 'what made me a Zionist was the Dreyfus trial'.[15] During the summer of 1893, he wrote *Der Judenstaat*, published in 1894. 'The message,' says O'Brien, 'was that there was no room or hope for Jews in Europe; that the Jews must acquire a territory on which to build a nation' (p. 71). The position is quite opposite to that of the Pittsburg Platform. Herzl was convinced that Jews should seek their own nation state. The idea was not welcomed by all Jews. Indeed in October 1917, Claude Montefiore, a leading British Jew, wrote to the British War Cabinet in a desperate effort to avert the Balfour Declaration. His national home was Britain and he wanted no other. 'It is very significant,' he said, 'that anti-semites are always very sympathetic to Zionism,' for it confirmed their claim that Jews were really aliens.[16]

The first Zionist Congress was convened by Herzl in Basel in 1897. During the years before the war, he gained support and was involved in various diplomatic moves, whilst pioneers continued to settle on the Land. It was, however, the Balfour Declaration in 1917 which gave a decisive impulse to the movement. Partly to gain advantage in the war situation, the British government declared that it 'viewed with favour' 'the establishment in Palestine of a national home for the Jewish people', but the government wanted it clearly understood that 'nothing shall be done which may prejudice the civil and religious rights of existing non-Jewish communities in Palestine'.[17]

1917–1947: British rule

Five weeks after the Balfour Declaration, on 9 December 1917, British forces took Jerusalem. The total population of Palestine at this time was about 512,000 Muslims, 61,000 Christians and 66,000 Jews.[18] For three years, Palestine was under British military rule, which was replaced in 1920 by a civilian administration. The first governor was Sir Herbert Samuel, of whom his biographer said he was 'the first Jewish ruler of Palestine since Hyrcanus II, that last degenerate Maccabean'.[19] The League of Nations mandate, finally agreed in 1923, under which Britain governed Palestine, included the terms of the Balfour Declaration. Implicit in them were inherent contradictions.

Conor Cruise O'Brien summarizes the contradictions within the Balfour Declaration between what 'His Majesty's Government "views with favour" – "the establishment in Palestine of a national home for the Jewish people" – and what it wants to be "clearly understood" – that "nothing shall be done which may prejudice the civil and religious rights of existing non-Jewish communities in Palestine . . ." In theory this contradiction is reconcilable in one of two ways. You could scale down the concept of a "national home" until it is indeed no longer felt to "prejudice the civil and religious rights", etc., of Arabs, as Arabs understood these rights, in which case the national home would turn out to be identical with the Old Yishuv, at most. Or you could scale down the concept of "civil and religious rights" for Arabs until these no longer conflict with the "national home", as envisaged by Zionists, in which case the civil and religious rights in question would – ultimately – be those guaranteed to Arabs by a Jewish state. In the first case, you would be doing the Jews out of what they thought they had been promised. In the second case, you would be doing the same to the Arabs' (p. 134).

These contradictions were reflected in changing British policy and in the different attitudes of members of the same adminis-tration. Up until 1929, the government, although not always fulfilling Zionist hopes, encouraged the national home. The sale of land to Zionists was allowed and visas were granted for legal Jewish immigration, which increased, partly because in 1924 the USA closed its gates to mass immigration. Many of the police and military, however, were unsympathetic to Jews – indeed they appeared to be so throughout the period of the Mandate. General Sir Arthur Money, the first Chief Administrator in Palestine, publicly rejected charges of antisemitism in the administration, but privately complained about 'Balfour, Lloyd George and their long-nosed friends'.[20] In 1921, General Congreve issued a circular to officers under his command, 'While the Army officially is supposed to have no politics, it is recognized that there are certain problems such as those of Ireland and Palestine in which the sympathies of the army are on one side or the other . . . In the case of Palestine these sympathies are rather obviously with the Arabs, who have hitherto appeared to the disinterested observer to have been the victim of the unjust policy forced upon them by the British government.'[21] After the Second World War, British forces were involved in turning back ships full of Holocaust survivors. In 1948, within two hundred yards of a British military post, seventy-seven doctors, nurses and students were murdered by Arabs. Although the attacks lasted for some seven hours, the British did nothing to intervene. Equally little was done to protect Arabs who were attacked by Jews in Haifa or elsewhere.

The Foreign Office, too, was consistently hostile to Jewish aspirations. For a time, from 1921, the position was eased for the Jews by the fact that Palestine was transferred from the Foreign Office to the Colonial Office and the defence of Palestine was placed under the Air Ministry.

In 1929, violence erupted – including cruel slaughter in Hebron. It had a profound effect. The hopes of those Jews who believed that a settlement acceptable to the Arabs could be found were discredited. As Vladimir Jabotinsky, a hardline leader, put it, 'There was no misunderstanding between Jew and Arab, but a natural conflict.'[22] Amongst the Jews in Israel there was a division between the political movement, known as Hagana, led by Ben Gurion, who was to become Israel's first prime minister, and the militant underground opposition to the Arabs, which became known as Irgun. At the same time the Yishuv became more self-reliant. Whilst still heavily dependent on World Zionism, the Yishuv no longer accepted the international leadership of World Zionism. There was also growing resentment against Britain. Amongst the Arabs the standing of Mufti Haj Amin was strengthened. He sought to reinforce the struggle against Zionism by giving it a religious dimension and preaching against Zionism in the mosques. He became increasingly anti-Jewish, so that during the war he ended up at Hitler's side. As for the British government, support for a national home cooled. The 1930 White Paper favoured an independent Arab Palestine, with guarantees for the Jews, but it came under heavy attack in Parliament and was dropped.

The early 1930s, with the rise of Hitler, meant a rapid increase of immigrants from just over 4,000 in 1931 to over 61,000 in 1935. By 1937 the Jewish population was 400,000. Meanwhile Arab resentment was growing and in 1936 erupted in the Arab Revolt – partly triggered by Britain's apparent weakness in failing to resist Mussolini's invasion of Ethiopia and Hitler's sending of troops into the demilitarized Rhineland. Because of a desire to gain Arab support in the event of a conflict with Hitler, Britain moved away from the idea of a national home for the Jews and now involved neighbouring Arab states in the complex situation. The 1937 Peel Commission recommended partition, but the Foreign Office disliked the idea and gained Prime Minister Chamberlain's support. In 1939, a White Paper was issued proposing, within ten years, an independent Palestine – technically secular but with an Arab majority. After five years, Jewish immigration would not be allowed, 'unless the Arabs of Palestine were prepared to acquiesce in it'.[23] Meanwhile a further 75,000 Jews would be admitted and adequate guarantees for the Jews would be required before independence would be granted. There was talk of Jewish revolt, but the Arabs themselves rejected the White Paper.

During the war, the Yishuv (the Jewish community) concentrated on helping the fight against the Nazis. With the end of hostilities, the British government stuck to the White Paper and despite strong pressure from President Truman refused to lift the ban on Jewish immigrants. This refusal was shown up in all its cruelty when the ship *Exodus* was refused permission to land. To make matters worse, it was also not allowed to disembark in Cyprus, so the victims of the Holocaust had to be taken back to the displaced persons camps in Germany, from which they had set out.

1947–1967: The birth of Israel

Soon afterwards a UN team reported and recommended the ending of the British mandate as soon as possible. It also recommended the partition of Palestine into an Arab and Jewish state, with an international zone in Jerusalem containing the Holy Places there. On 29 November 1947 this was accepted by the UN – although the Foreign Office had assumed that by referring the matter to the UN, all decisions would be stalled. The decision had the support of both USA and USSR. Britain abstained. Rather than stay and try to effect an orderly hand-over, the British government washed its hands of the situation – although it continued the Mandate until the following May. Both sides claimed that the British army favoured their opponents in these critical months.

On 14 May 1948, the day before the Mandate expired, Ben Gurion proclaimed the State of Israel. Eleven minutes later, as had been previously agreed with Weizmann, President Truman announced the United States' *de facto* recognition of Israel. Almost immediately five Arab states attacked Israel. Egyptian planes bombed Tel Aviv and Ben Gurion's first broadcast, as Prime Minister of Israel, was from an air-raid shelter. The Foreign Office and the British Chiefs of Staff reported categorically that the Arabs would throw the Jews into the sea.[24]

In fact, after a desperate struggle for survival, by the time the armistices were signed in 1949, Israel had gained about one-third more territory than the UN partition plan had allowed for. It had also gained West Jerusalem, so that Jerusalem was now a city divided between Jews and Arabs. Israel, which was absorbing Jewish refugees from Arab lands, made it clear that it would not take back the Arab refugees, who had fled because of the war and especially because of the terror created by the Deir Yassin massacre. Argument continues whether the Arabs were encouraged to flee by the Arab powers and whether Israeli authorities urged them to stay. During the fighting, King Abdullah of Transjordan occupied the area designated for the Arab state and also moved into the Old City and East Jerusalem. It is important, when there is talk of a Palestinian state, to remember that from 1948–1967, as a result of conquest, the West Bank was part of Jordan. The legitimacy of all boundaries that emerged – in terms of the UN partition plan – are questionable. The hope of an international corridor for Jerusalem and a *corpus separatum* also disappeared, although the Vatican clung to such a hope for many years.

At first there was some hope of peace or at least of an

understanding between Israel and King Abdullah, but he was soon assassinated. There were it seems, some secret contacts, but they proved abortive, as have all such hopes of peace with Jordan. During its early years, the state of Israel absorbed a large number of Oriental Jews. The early fifties was also a time of isolation as the USA cultivated Arab friends. Terrorist or *fedayeen* raids from Egypt caused growing loss of life. In 1955, there were 238 casualties. Israel determined to hit back and saw its opportunity in the Suez crisis when Britain and France attempted unsuccessfully to recover control of the Suez Canal. Egypt's army was broken, but America's fury meant that Israel could not keep its gains, although a UN force was positioned to stop *fedayeen* attacks.

1967–1982

The decade after Suez was a period of growth, progress and relative calm. Then in 1967, in the Six Day War, caused by the growing hostility of the surrounding Arab states, Israeli troops overran the West Bank and Sinai and captured the whole of Jerusalem. In the subsequent UN debates, the famous Resolution 242 was passed unanimously. It called for:

(i) Withdrawal of Israeli armed forces from territories occupied in the recent conflict.
(ii) Termination of all claims or states of belligerency and respect for and acknowledgement of the sovereignty, territorial integrity and political independence of every State in the area, and their right to live in peace within secure and recognized boundaries.[25]

Israel accepted the resolution, but by making clear the linkage between the two paragraphs. 'There was a clear understanding that it was only within the establishment of permanent peace with secure and recognized boundaries that the other principles could be given effect.'[26] The representative of Syria also made clear that he understood the resolution in this sense, although subsequently Arab spokesmen repudiated this. Thus Israel and the Arab powers have refused to take action until both sides initiate action to fulfil the resolution.

Another complication was that the English text spoke of territories, not *the* territories, so Israel was to claim that it was required to evacuate *some* but not all the territories in question. Russian does not have a definite article and the French text included the definite article: but it was the original English text that Israel accepted.

Initially there was a willingness to trade land for peace: but only some land. Israel wanted secure and recognized boundaries and the pre–1967 boundaries were in places hard to defend, especially the narrow coastal strip north of Tel Aviv. The 1973 Yom Kippur war, in which Israel was surprised and for a moment came dangerously near to defeat, emphasized the need for extra land for its own security. Yet, prompted by the American Secretary of State Henry Kissinger, it was still willing to make concessions. Another effect of the war, however, was to hasten the electors' disillusionment with the Labour Party which was blamed for being unprepared and also for its corruption. The 1977 election for the first time brought to power Likud, which wished to hold on to 'Judaea and Samaria', which it regarded as an integral part of the Promised Land. Jewish settlements in the area increased, despite protest from the international community.

Yet it was Menahem Begin, the Likud prime minister, who seized the olive branch offered by President Sadat of Egypt. In November 1977, Sadat came to Jerusalem to address the Knesset. As Begin said in reply, 'The flight time between Cairo and Jerusalem is short, but the distance between Cairo and Jerusalem was until last night almost endless.'[27] The following year, thanks to President Jimmy Carter's persistence, peace was reached at Camp David. Israel agreed to withdraw from Sinai. The position of the Palestinians was left for further consideration on the basis of a suggestion of local autonomy. Egypt now became isolated from other Arab nations.

From the war in Lebanon to the present day

If there was now peace on the Egyptian border, Palestinian Liberation Organization (PLO) attacks were increasing in the north from Lebanon, where the PLO were now entrenched. These attacks were also fomenting unrest on the West Bank. The Soviet Union, too, was giving Syria missiles, which could threaten Israel. In 1986, with the tacit assent of the USA,[28] Israel struck at the PLO in Lebanon and soon had taken control of East Beirut. But then West Beirut was besieged and in August the PLO were evacuated. Not content with evicting the PLO, Israel tried to establish hegemony over Lebanon by setting up a pro-Israeli president, Bashir Gemayel.

This was too much for Syria, and soon the world was to be appalled
by the massacres carried out by Christian Phalangists, unchecked by
Israel, at the camps of Sabra and Chatila. The grief at the massacre –
together with his wife's death and his illness – led to Begin
withdrawing into seclusion and he let it be known that he felt
betrayed by Ariel Sharon, his Minister of Defence. Begin presumably genuinely believed that Israeli troops entering West Beirut
would 'prevent any possible incident and secure quiet'.[29] Sharon, it
seems, had other and more ruthless plans.

In the aftermath of Sabra and Chatila, Israel agreed to withdraw its
forces from Beirut. It is perhaps worth noting that it was Israeli
journalists who first made known what had happened and that a full
government enquiry was held. Already the Lebanon war was
unpopular with many Israelis and with Jewish friends elsewhere. It
was the first obviously aggressive war launched by Israel. It was
covered by television, which showed horrific scenes in Beirut, where
the PLO fighters lived amidst civilians. Many of the PLO bases were
in refugee camps, but news of the bombing of refugee camps shocked
many in the West. The campaign did succeed in ensuring that there
was no longer an autonomous PLO with a territorial base anywhere
on Israel's frontiers – the remaining sections of the PLO were under
Syrian control – and it was an understandable objective. Attempts,
however, to turn Lebanon into an Israeli puppet state were bound to
provoke Syria. What was achieved, too, was at a high price in terms of
Israeli lives and resources (as well as Palestinian lives). It also led to
deep divisions within Israel and loss of sympathy in world opinion.
Indeed Israelis found themselves likened to the Nazis, so that
Nicholas Von Hoffman wrote in *The Spectator* that 'Americans are
coming to see the Israeli Government as pounding the Star of David
into a swastika'[30].

After Sabra and Chatila, Israel withdrew its forces to a buffer zone.
The 1984 election resulted in a hung parliament, with a so-called
government of national unity. Shimon Peres was Prime Minister for
two years and Yitzhak Shamir for the second two-year term. They
made little effort to disguise their disagreements on foreign policy or
settlements in the West Bank. Shamir and his Likud party were
committed to retaining Judaea and Samaria, whilst Peres was
prepared to take part in an international conference and was willing
to trade land for peace, but was not prepared to deal with the PLO
nor to accept a Palestinian state.

In 1988, another election left Mr Shamir as head of another government of national unity, which is still deeply divided on foreign policy. As I write, in the summer of 1989, the prolonged *infatada* uprising on the West Bank and Gaza strip shows no signs of abating. The harsh measures used by the Israeli army to repress the uprising have even further alienated the sympathy of world opinion from Israel. Jordan has withdrawn its interest and the PLO has set up a government in exile and given clearer signs of recognizing Israel's existence.

What hope of peace?

To the outside world, any hope of peace seems to depend on Israel's being willing to evacuate a large part of the occupied territories and allowing Palestinian self-determination. The likelihood of this, however, remains small. It would require an Israeli government strong enough to deliver. It is in any case unlikely that any Israeli government would give up enough land to satisfy the Arabs and suggestions of local autonomy are unlikely to be acceptable to the Palestinians. No conceivable Israeli government would surrender Jerusalem, claims to which, as the third most holy city for Muslims, Arabs could never abandon. Even in the West Bank any Israeli government would want to retain land to make for secure boundaries. Israelis too have consistently refused to negotiate with the PLO, but there are no other Palestinians with the authority to negotiate, especially now Jordan has withdrawn its interests.

Even if Israel negotiated with the PLO, could Israel accept a Palestinian state? Would Palestinians be content with it or would it be a springboard for further action? Many in the West assume that the PLO is really willing to drop its threats to destroy Israel and would now settle for a West Bank state, but can recent declarations be taken at face value? This may be true of Palestinians in the area, but such a decision would split the PLO. Even so-called 'moderate' PLO are shown to have been involved in terrorist action. It is questionable whether a West Bank Palestinian state would be economically viable unless linked to Jordan, which now seems a less likely option, especially as Syria too has ambitions in the area. Of course the pressure of the super powers, if they were to act together, and international guarantees might force both Israelis and Palestinians to agree and failure to do so seems to the outsider damaging to both. Certainly the long occupation of the West Bank and Gaza is harmful to Israel's own democracy, oppressive to the Arab inhabitants and is increasing the alienation of the Arab citizens who live in pre-1967 Israel.

If it is hard to see Israel making concessions adequate to satisfy the Palestinians, their miserable plight looks likely to continue. The dominant Israeli view is that only harshness will eventually subdue the Arabs and make them come to terms with the reality of Israel. Improvements – and before the recent uprising there had been considerable economic and material improvements – are now likely to be thought of as concessions and a sign of weakness. Some extreme Israelis, of course, like Rabbi Kahane, hope that eventually Arabs will leave the area, especially as Jewish settlements continue. Others work for reconciliation and peace.[31] Yet just as white expansion in Australasia has been unfair to Aboriginals and Maoris, so the Jewish homeland has caused injustice and suffering to the Arabs. It is difficult to see how this could have been avoided, given the premises on which Zionism was based. It is difficult to see how further Arab suffering can be avoided whilst Palestinians, abetted by Arab propaganda but little practical help, retain ambitions which have little hope of realization.

Too often outsiders are unaware of the complexity of the situation and its deep tragedy. Moral exhortations are resented by Israel, especially from members of nations which partly caused the tragedy. Israeli actions are judged more harshly than those of neighbouring Arab states. There was scarcely a mention by the Western press of the Syrian massacre of thousands of its own citizens at Hama. This is because Israel is a democracy and judged in the West by democratic standards.

The tragedy is that almost all involved are prisoners of history. Perhaps only when all involved recognize that the tragedy is not of their making but that they are victims of it may some of the bitterness and blame ease and the possibility of finding a *modus vivendi* may emerge in which no one gets all they want but which allows the young to grow up in peace. Whilst Palestinians retain unreal expectations, they bolster those in Israel who refuse any concession. Sadly some of the Palestinians' vocal supporters outside encourage them in their unreal expectations.

3. Christian responses

Most churches have a presence in the Holy Land, and apart from ex-patriates, the Christians are mostly Arab. Whilst they recognize that Christians from Western Europe and the USA feel guilty about the Holocaust, they sometimes feel resentful that this seems to be expressed in uncritical support of Israel. Both sides claim that Christian comment is one-sided.

Some indeed see the Christian role as 'advocacy' – speaking for those who suffer injustice. Some who felt called to speak for Jews and Israel before 1967, now feel called to speak for the Palestinians. Sometimes in doing the latter, they use emotive language, which inflames the situation. To speak of events on the West Bank as 'a holocaust', or to compare Israeli actions with South African (with the implication that Zionism is a racist policy comparable to apartheid) naturally makes Jews defensive and hinders the work of Jewish moderates. Is it that Christians want to suggest that the 'Jewish state' behaves as badly as so-called 'Christian' states?

Christian comment reflects the variety of Christian attitudes to Israel. Some see in the return of the Jews the working of God and perhaps a fulfilment of prophecies which suggest the End is near.[32] A group of Christian leaders in Israel, in a recent statement, say: 'There is a sizeable body of Christian opinion in the world – and we are among them – who believe that the return of the Jewish people to their ancestral homeland has been under God's hand. This does not give Israel a *carte blanche* to behave as it likes. But it does mean that their return to the land of their fathers has been in accordance with God's Word and will.'[33] Sometimes fundamentalist groups who identify closely with Israel also expect the conversion of the Jews before the Messiah returns. Others, dissociating themselves from messianic expectations and eschatological speculations, see the return of the Jews 'as a sign of God's faithfulness towards His people'.[34] Others, whilst affirming the existence of Israel, see this as a political reality to be understood in terms of international law, with no particular theological meaning. The statement of the General Assembly of the Presbyterian Church (USA), for example, says: 'The State of Israel is a geopolitical entity and is not to be validated theologically.'[35] This seems to be the position of the Vatican, which still does not recognize the state of Israel. Others, especially those who have worked with Palestinian refugees, believe that Christians are called to stand with the oppressed Palestinians.[36]

The Christian is in no position to lecture or to adopt a high moral tone. He or she needs to appreciate the complexity of the situation and to support all who are working for peace and understanding. It seems better to try to help those who have been hurt and wronged to listen and recognize that others are hurting too, than to reinforce them in their bitterness by uncritical advocacy of their cause. The Christian from outside must beware of inflaming passions, and the role, it seems to me, is that of conciliator, not advocate. There is a need to protest at violations of human rights, by whomsoever they are perpetrated. We do this, however, as humans and not as Christians – affirming rights recognized by the United Nations and, it is to be hoped, by all people of faith and goodwill.

Above all, the Christian needs to approach the tragic situation with penitence, especially if the Christian is British. European antisemitism and Christian anti-Judaism have partly caused the problem and British policy was often self-serving.

4. Conclusion

Nowhere have I felt more strongly than in Israel and the West Bank the need for forgiveness and nowhere recognized more clearly its cost. All have been hurt, and a new beginning is only possible when that hurt can be accepted and people are willing to make themselves vulnerable to others. Mordechai Bar-on, a spokesperson for Peace Now, who was elected to the Knesset in 1984, admits that he has killed Arabs. But his daughter married a Palestinian Arab, 'a Muslim whom I love'. 'Of course,' he says, 'both sides have done a lot of bad, criminal things to each other, but on the whole I cannot and do not want to repent for the Zionist project.' He accepts, however, that 'a basic wrong was done to the Palestinians. When they will accept that I cannot be but who I am, a Zionist living a Jewish existence in this land, then I will go down on my knees and ask for their forgiveness.'[37] Mustafa Natshe, the deposed Mayor of Hebron, repeatedly quotes a verse from the Qur'an, 'God created you as nations and tribes in order to understand each other – not to quarrel but understand.'[38] There are those who work for under-standing and they must be strengthened in this.

In the suffering of the Jewish and Palestinian people, we see again the suffering of God, which can move us to discover a oneness in

which our particularity is affirmed and not threatened and in which
we grant to others the dignity we seek for ourselves.

A Muslim poet, Ysuf al-Khal, drawing on Jewish and Christian
images, voices the pain of the people:

> Thirsty? Take the rock and strike it.
> Tombed in darkness? Roll away the stone from the grave.
> When hunger takes you, here is your manna,
> Your solace.
> Naked you have become? Then take fig leaves
> For a robe to cover the evil and hide it
> From the sight of men.
> And in the great temptation take to yourself
> The patience of Job, and, when evil is overwhelming,
> Do not fall into despair.
> The cross of God is raised
> On the hill of this present world.'[39]

But again the haunting question comes, 'Is non-violent forgiving
love strong enough in face of the evil, pain and bitterness of the
world?' Another Arab poet, Kamal Nasir, sounds a chilling note:

> Apostle of forgiveness,
> Dazed by disaster, I do not know the answer:
> Is it true you lived to suffer?
> Is it true you came to redeem?
> Apostle of forgiveness, in our tragedy
> Neither forgiveness nor love avail.[40]

To see Israelis and Palestinians as prisoners of a tragic history
may quicken outside sympathy and remove the temptation to make
snap judgments and moral pronouncements. Only as both sides
realize that both have been hurt and that further conflict will
increase the hurt will they perhaps be willing to forego their dreams
and to discover a *modus vivendi*. For that to happen, outside powers
need genuinely to seek the peace of the region rather than use the
inhabitants as pawns in their political ambitions. Meanwhile those
who long for the peace of Jerusalem must eschew and challenge all
propaganda and pray and support those who struggle for reconciliation. Work for peace anywhere is hard; nowhere is it harder
than in Jerusalem. No wonder many believe that when peace comes
to Jerusalem, it will be also 'for the healing of the nations'.

12

A Shared Responsibility

One of my sadnesses about the Middle East has been the failure of
Jewish, Muslim and Christian religious leaders to be heard speaking
clearly in the name of peace and justice. In the 1960s, my friend
Albert Polack, Housemaster of the Jewish house at Clifton College,
Bristol and for a time Education Secretary of CCJ, wrote to the
papers appealing for such a joint approach on the basis of the ethical
values shared by the three Abrahamic faiths. There have been
various attempts at trilateral conversations and joint work for
reconciliation, but these initiatives have been voluntary and
unofficial.

At CCJ, I helped to set up an Israel Advisory Group to see
whether there could be a growth of understanding between some
Jews and Christians about attitudes to Israel. The attempt to
broaden the group to include some Christians with deep sympathies
for the Palestinians proved too difficult. Even in Britain, well away
from the scene of conflict, people came as advocates of one position
and were unwilling to try to hear the other points of view. I was
reminded of the discussion on Afghanistan at the WCC Assembly
in Vancouver in 1983. Listening to the debate, it seemed that all
who spoke echoed the views of their respective governments. It did
not appear that there was a specific Christian message.

The hope that there might be a distinctive religious witness for
peace and justice has been a continuing motivation of the inter-faith
movement. Soon after the outbreak of the Second World War, Sir
Francis Younghusband said: 'A new world order is now the dream
of men, but for this a new spirit will be needed. This is the special
concern of men of religion, in this case of all religions.'[1] Since 1977
this has been the aim of the World Conference on Religion and

Peace. When, too, CCJ was formed in Britain in 1942, one of the aims was to promote the fundamental ethical teachings common to both religions. Whilst this aim has never been forgotten, the immediate priorities were education and overcoming bitterness, so as to build up the trust necessary for such shared endeavour. NCCJ in the USA has, perhaps, been more active in the field of community relations.

There are signs that the suffering and injustice of the world are at last prompting members of world religions to work together. The energy of the pioneers of the inter-faith movement were largely devoted to encouraging people of different faiths to meet on a basis of understanding and goodwill. Prejudices had to be dispelled and theological hesitations overcome. Now there is increasing contact on matters of urgent concern to society. Yet the fact that this is the shortest chapter shows how little has yet been achieved.

A beginning is being made. In 1984 representatives of all major religions shared in a United Nations Inter-faith Colloquium against Apartheid, chaired by Bishop Trevor Huddleston. In 1988, one hundred religious and political leaders, including the Dalai Lama and Mother Teresa, met together at Oxford for the Global Forum on Human Survival. It became clear that the environmental crisis requires both political wisdom and spiritual insights. Earlier in 1986, religious leaders met at Assisi to voice their concern for the environment, at a gathering arranged by the World Wildlife Fund. Religious leaders speaking together may help to change public opinion.

Significantly, the 1987 second official international Anglican–Jewish consultation did not dwell on past problems. Chaired by the Archbishop of York and the Chief Rabbi, it concentrated on what the two communities could say and do together about the major social issues of the inner cities and the threat of Aids. On the inner cities, the concluding statement said: 'Concerned about the injustices of multiple deprivation in urban priority areas, we believe that responses are required from our religious communities. There is a vigorous debate within both communities on the practical responses that should be made. The Consultation enabled us to discover the substantial similarity in the nature of the debates in both communities. On the strength of our discussions we believe there is a sufficient measure of agreement among us to engage in co-operative efforts. We therefore urge the Christian and Jewish communities, both locally and nationally, to develop means of continued consultation and practical co-operation.'[2]

Yet are religious people sufficiently agreed to be able to say anything together or to make a common witness? Will any agreed statement be so general and platitudinous as to be worthless? Or are religions being used to bolster up values which do not derive from them but from liberal or social democracy?

Internal disagreements

Certainly there are disagreements within most traditions. Christians are divided on whether a war can be just or whether it is moral for a nation to possess nuclear weapons. They disagree about contraception and abortion. The Jewish and Muslim traditions have a more positive attitude than Christians to honest wealth-creation. For many centuries, an ascetic tradition has inhibited Christian enjoyment of sexuality in a way not found in Judaism or Islam.

The possibility of broadening the debate has been shown in the Jewish–Christian conversations about the inner city and Aids. At the invitation of the Archbishop of Canterbury, the Chief Rabbi responded to the influential Anglican report *Faith in the City* with a pamphlet *From Doom to Hope*. In this he compared the Jewish and the black experience in Britain. 'We worked on ourselves, not on others . . . We made ourselves highly acceptable and indispensable by our industrial, intellectual and moral contributions to society.'[3] He mentioned, too, respect for the police as a minority's safeguard, and wrote that Jews never demanded that British society should change its own character.

The views of the Chief Rabbi, who is perceived by the British public to represent British Jewry, although he only speaks for Orthodox Jews, were sharply criticized by other Jews, mainly members of the Reform and Progressive communities. They argued that many in the black community were victims of circumstance and discrimination, not their own failure. It was clear, too, that the Chief Rabbi put less stress on structural and economic factors than the authors of the report. He also insisted on the value of work. 'No work is too menial to compromise human dignity and self-respect . . . Idleness is an even greater evil than unemployment.' The report, he wrote, 'falls short of hailing work as a virtue in itself'.[4]

The discussion of Aids and homosexuality has also shown deep differences within both church and synagogue. Leaders of both religions have rejected the suggestion that Aids is a punishment of God. The area of disagreement is whether modern knowledge should modify traditional condemnation of homosexuality. 'The Jewish view,' wrote the Chief Rabbi, 'is plain and uncompromising. All the authentic sources of Judaism condemn homosexual relations as a heinous offence.'[5] The Liberal rabbi David Goldberg, however, said he was willing to modify biblical and rabbinical teachings in the light of modern knowledge about human sexuality, 'which suggests that for some people homosexuality is their "natural" sexual orientation'.[6] There is a similar argument amongst Christian writers on the subject, which points to differences about the authority on which moral judgments are based. To what extent is moral teaching determined by scripture or may that scripture be interpreted in the light of new knowledge?

The *Humanum*

At the level of scripture, religions may not agree. Is it possible, however, by sharing our understanding of the human vocation – of what it means for a person to be made in the image of God – to find a meeting point? Hans Küng has asked, 'Should it not be possible, *by appealing to the common humanity in all people*, to formulate a universal ethical, truly *ecumenical basic criterion* that rests on the *Humanum*, the *truly human*, concretely on *human dignity* and the *basic values* associated with it? The fundamental ethical question can be formulated: What is good for human beings? The answer: what helps them to be what is not so easily defined: an authentic human person! Accordingly the basic ethical criterion is: Humans should not live inhumanly, bestially, but should live like humans, true humans, humanely.'[7] The criterion for what is good and true in religion is therefore what serves humanity. The criterion acts also as a critique of religion. Küng points out that 'progress towards humaneness within all the various religions – despite all the lags in consciousness – is unmistakeable since their entrance into the modern world: Consider the abolition of the inquisitorial practices of fire and torture, customary within Roman Catholicism until well into the modern age; the elimination of human sacrifice and widow-burning, which was practised in scattered areas of India – although never by Buddhists or Christians – into the period of the

British occupation; a new, more humane interpretation of the doctrine of "Holy War", and reforms of the penal laws in the more progressive Islamic countries . . .' (p. 13).

Yet although the *Humanum* serves as a critique of religion, it is undergirded by religion. 'In the battle for the *Humanum*, religion is able to explain unambiguously what politics cannot explain: why morality, ethical values and norms must bind unconditionally (and not only when I find them comfortable) and also universally (for all strata, classes and races). The *Humanum* is saved by being linked to the divine. For is it not true? Only the Unconditioned itself can obligate unconditionally, only the Absolute can bind absolutely, only the ultimate can bind ultimately' (p. 13).

Küng, therefore, suggests:

(1) True *humanity* is the *presupposition for true religion!* That is, the *Humanum* (the respect for human dignity and basic values) is a minimal demand on every religion: there must be at least humaneness (this is a minimal criterion) if there is to be genuine religion.

(2) True *religion* is the *completion of true humanity!* That is, religion (as an expression of comprehensive meaning, of highest values, of unconditional obligation) is an optimal presupposition for the realization of the *Humanum*: there must be religion (this is a maximal criterion) if there is to be humaneness as an unconditioned and universal obligation (p. 15).

Dr Michael Ramsey, who was Archbishop of Canterbury, and David Jenkins, the Bishop of Durham, have claimed that Christianity – and its ethical teaching derives from Judaism – is the true humanism, in the sense that it points to abundant life and human fulfilment and that its moral teaching is for the true welfare of men and women.[8]

This suggests that beyond the differences about moral behaviour that exist, religious thinkers could be encouraged to share their visions of authentic human life – of 'man in the image of God', of a human being freed from *avidya* or ignorance. If such visions are genuinely derived from the scriptural authorities of a tradition, then they are not just an expression of the values of the moment. It suggests also that moral teaching is not just a matter of quoting texts dealing with a particular topic, but of deriving such teaching from the overall understanding of the relationship of the human to the divine contained in the tradition.

Despite the differences between and within religious traditions, it is possible to hope that there may be a coming together in the human values which the different religions affirm. All, for example, affirm the sacredness of life and human dignity. Some of the commonalities between religions have been noted by Professor Halsey in a contribution to work by the European Value Systems Study Group. He uses results of a sample together with a study by Dr John Bowker. Bowker argued for some commonalities between Christianity and five other faiths, namely 'the centrality of prayer to religious practice, the significance of individual life as a balance of virtue and vice determining a fate beyond death, the insignificance of individual life in the pages of eternity, the rootedness of religious belief in family continuity, and the ultimate belief in one God'. This, Halsey argues, 'seems capable of translation into a common ethical creed of love, hope and charity, binding a nation and extending towards all, even all creation'.[9]

Religious communities are only now ceasing to view one another as rivals and recognizing one another as children of one God, although in all communities there is an opposing increase of intolerance and extremism.

Those who see the importance of dialogue should now, I believe, concentrate on the practical contribution that they can make to the whole society. Together, I hope, they will affirm certain fundamental values derived from their shared view of the dignity and sanctity of life. At the same time, the variety of the particular experiences and traditions should enrich society as we come to value the otherness of the other as much as our common humanity. It is a contribution which Jews and Christians, whose ethical teachings go back to the same sources, are especially fitted to make. Indeed many who hesitate about 'theological dialogue' may be willing to support this more practical co-operation.

13

Together to Pray

All conferences are full of talk, but at the first International Council of Christians and Jews Colloquium (ICCJ) that I attended, I was surprised that there was no silence. In inter-faith gatherings with Hindus or Buddhists, there is usually at least some silence early in the morning. In personal relationships, silence is only embarrassing if we do not know the other person well. Perhaps at that stage not all members of ICCJ were sufficiently trusting of one another to be together in the presence of God. Jews naturally are very wary of covert Christian evangelism or even the imposition of Christian assumptions. The lack of silence masked the lack of trust. Similarly, in a group of clergy and rabbis who have met regularly for some time, it was only after three years that the possibility of some time together in the acknowledged presence of God was first discussed. It is easier to talk about God than to be together before God. It is important to establish trust in a group before venturing far in being together to pray.

Gradually a pattern of 'spiritual sharing' has evolved at ICCJ meetings, so that whilst there is the opportunity to offer the prayers of each particular community of faith, there is also time to reflect together, to listen to inspiring readings, to sing together and to be quiet together. This development, in my view, has led to a deepening of the life of ICCJ.

The possibility of being together in prayer underlines the spiritual search at the heart of inter-faith exploration, which, in the words of America's first All-Faiths Chapel, is 'dedicated to the spirit of human unity and the universality of the quest for the Highest'.[1] Religions meet, it has been said, where religions take their source, in God.

I recall one of my first visits to Jerusalem. In the afternoon, I had been to the Western Wall as a tourist. Later that day, I visited a Jewish friend. In the evening we drove round the old city and when we came near to the Western Wall, we stopped and walked to it. She went up to the wall and inserted a tiny scroll with the name of a loved one for whom she wished to pray. I was privileged to be there and felt caught up in her communion with the Holy One. On another visit, a rabbi friend asked me to go there with him for the welcoming of the sabbath. On both occasions, I was a guest at another's moment of prayer and shared a little of their experience and in so doing was brought closer to them.

Yet such meeting in the Spirit is very difficult, especially in any formal or public way, as it is thought to threaten traditional loyalties. For many Christians it calls in question their assumptions that God has uniquely revealed himself to them. To lessen hesitations it is important, therefore, to stress that such coming together to pray is not a substitute for the regular worship or liturgy of a religious community. It may reduce misunderstanding to avoid speaking of 'inter-faith worship' or 'inter-faith services'.

Each community has its own pattern of prayer. Orthodox Jewish prayer requires a *minyan* of ten males and follows an inherited tradition. Christian prayer is 'through Jesus Christ our Lord'. In any community there are shared assumptions of belief, as well as accepted patterns of behaviour. Affirming the integrity and distinctiveness of a faith community is important in developing closer relationships between communities. For if a community feels threatened, it is likely to withdraw. At a personal level, many of us need to be nourished in our own community of faith.

Guests

Yet there are occasions when we are guests at another's prayers. Synagogues are usually very hospitable and members of other faiths are normally welcome to attend synagogue services. If they are orthodox synagogues, however, the service will be almost entirely in Hebrew. On the Saturday of the first CCJ Conference that I attended in the early 1960s, we all went to the Orthodox morning service. It lasted more than two hours and most of the Christians were not able to follow. There was no explanation or commentary. Yet to add such is to alter the tradition. Do we, when guests are present, allow for them or maintain the integrity of the liturgy? I recall attending what had been billed as an 'All Faiths Service', which proved to be Anglican evensong. Although guests of other faiths had been invited, the priest when it came to the creed said, 'We shall now all stand and say the creed'. The rabbi, next to whom I was sitting, muttered, 'A bit difficult for some of us'. It seems reasonable when guests are present to acknowledge them and to explain our own customs and traditions.

It is more debatable whether we modify the service because we have guests with us. Do you continue to conclude prayers with 'through Jesus Christ Our Lord'? It would be disastrous to invite Jewish friends and then read as the lesson either Matthew 23, with its repeated, 'Alas for you, lawyers and Pharisees, hypocrites', or John 8, with its words, 'Your father is the devil'.

Indeed, if we are embarrassed to read these passages with Jews present, we should not be reading them in public worship. Much anti-Jewish liturgical material, such as the Good Friday Reproaches, has been purged or dropped. It is not so easy to know what to do with polemical scripture. Krister Stendahl wrote of a Gospel of St John he received which stated on the title page, 'This is the Gospel according to Saint John, in the words of the King James Version of the year 1611. Edited in conformity with the true ecumenical spirit of His Holiness, Pope John XXIII, by Dagobert D. Runes. The message of Jesus is offered here without adulteration by hate and revulsion against the people of the Savior.' Some twenty passages from the Fourth Gospel had been cut out. At other points references to 'the Jews' are replaced by general terms such as 'the people' or 'the crowd'. Although the intention is laudable, as Krister Stendahl says, 'it is hard to believe that the production of a fraudulent text can help anyone'.[2] Whilst the choice of readings or production of lectionaries needs to be done with care, perhaps even more important is to encourage an awareness of the benefits of a critical approach to scripture.[3]

A number of Jews still feel a strong emotional reaction on entering a church, because they will be reminded of centuries of persecution and anti-Judaism. I recall a Jewish–Christian event which was being arranged in a church. Those present, many of whom would be Jews, would be facing the pulpit on which there was a large crucifix. Some Jews wondered whether the crucifix might be veiled for the occasion. The church authorities felt this might be misinterpreted by their fellow believers as apologizing for the faith.

In the end, the lectern was used instead as the focus and a large vase of flowers was put in front of the pulpit.

At another CCJ conference, it had been agreed that we should encourage people to attend a typical act of worship of each faith, rather than specially arranged services. On the Sunday, Jewish members of the conference were invited to the eucharist in the conference chapel. At the last minute, I was asked to preach. The Gospel for the day included Jesus' question, 'Who do you say that I am?' and Peter's confession, 'You are the Messiah, the Son of the Living God' (Matt. 15.16). My initial reaction was to think of changing the reading, but I hesitantly decided that it was important to speak of where Jews and Christians agreed and disagreed.

The presence of guests of another faith does alter the dynamics of traditional worship, and I feel their presence needs to be acknowledged – at least by some explanation of what is happening. If there is material which might cause offence and which cannot be omitted, again, explanation helps, and the acknowledgment that it might cause offence shows sensitivity to the guests. It needs also to be made clear that the guests are there initially as observers and it is for them to decide the extent to which they may also be participants. Invitations to speak, perhaps to read or to join in singing psalms or certain hymns, may be appreciated, but any pressure is to be avoided.

Life situations

Life situations demand a creative response. A Jewish lady whose Christian husband had just died asked whether I would take the funeral and whether her rabbi could also take part. I agreed, and he, although aware of likely criticism, said he would read a psalm. In the vestry, before the service, he could not decide whether or not to robe. Would that make him an officiant? Eventually he did robe and beside the psalm he read a prayer by John Donne, the seventeenth-century poet and Dean of St Paul's Cathedral, which begins 'Bring us, O Lord, at our last awakening . . .' Afterwards the widow told me that when they married, there was no minister or rabbi prepared to say a blessing for them, and because her husband was divorced, he was not allowed communion. At another funeral of the daughter of a mixed marriage, I was invited to speak during the synagogue service.

Religious provision for 'mixed marriages' is very difficult. For Jews, who are a small minority in Britain, 'marrying out' weakens the community. It is feared, with good grounds, that the one who marries

out will give up his or her Jewish observance and may not bring up
the children as Jews. (Only children of a Jewish mother are Jews.)
Christians often express similar fears that the Christian partner's
faith will be diluted. Too often, however, religious rules seem to
deny human need. The negative reaction which is common may
turn people away from traditional faith.

I am conscious that my response to a few couples who have
approached me has been experimental. Some years ago, a young
couple asked whether I would bless their marriage. The girl, an
American, was the daughter of conservative Jews. She herself was
not observant, but had taken up Yoga. The young man had been
brought up as a member of the Church of England, but had joined
the Divine Light Mission. They had met on a religious studies
course! For taking the service, which was a moving and special
occasion, I was given a copy of the Aquarian Gospel. I have also
taken a service at which a non-observant Jew married a Christian
girl. He was content to take part in a Christian service, but made his
promises in the name of God and was not asked to make any
christological statements. Another Jew, who was not himself
observant, did not feel that his family would be prepared to come to
a service in a church. He suggested the possibililty of a neutral
venue or of beginning the reception with some prayers and
readings.

There is no clear precedent for these new situations, and in
Britain, at any rate, experiments are circumscribed by the requirements of the marriage laws. Hardly any rabbis in Britain are
willing to take part in a 'mixed' occasion, although some liberal
Rabbis in the USA may be willing to do so. (The legal position in
the two countries is different.)

Clearly a couple from different faiths, even more than from
different denominations, need to appreciate each other's beliefs
and respect their integrity. Too easily they can adopt a position of
relativism and indifference. But in marriage, we learn to respect the
otherness of the other and such respect is essential for our global
society. Where this exists, there can be a deep and creative
relationship, as many successful 'mixed' marriages bear witness.
Whilst couples should be made fully aware of the difficulties, it
saddens me that our religious communities offer very little pastoral
support to those of different faith who truly love each other. Often
they are made to feel rejection when they most need help and

encouragement. Our pastoral care, as well as our theology, needs to adjust to our new appreciation of the bonds that unite Jews and Christians.

Together to pray

There are a growing number of other occasions when members of different faiths share deeply, perhaps at a conference or meeting for dialogue, where some knowledge and a depth of personal relationships may be assumed. The London Rainbow group for Christian–Jewish dialogue begins with the reading of a psalm. The CCJ executive meeting starts with a short time of silence – when most people hunt for their agendas!

Easily, however, anything done jointly may become characterless. All Faiths services are sometimes just a series of readings with very generalized hymns. No one is offended, but perhaps also no one is uplifted. It is more valuable to try to draw out the universal meaning embodied in almost every tradition. One of the most memorable inter-faith services in which I participated was at the West London Synagogue, when the Dalai Lama preached there. The ceremony included the Torah procession and reading from the scroll. This was followed by other readings. The occasion allowed visitors to feel a little of the beauty of Jewish worship and to bring their own offering to this.

On other occasions, the symbolism of light, the giving of flowers or the greeting of peace has been used. Our contemporary situation of increasing inter-faith contact needs a new and creative response and the discovery of appropriate symbols. This helps to emphasize that what is being done is new for a new situation and not a tinkering with time-honoured traditions of worship. The integrity of a faith community is not being called in question, but the importance of faith communities relating creatively to each other is being affirmed.[4]

A significant development, especially in the USA, is the growing number of Christian congregations who observe Holocaust Remembrance Day (Yom Hashoah), sometimes together with Jews. The practice started in the early 1970s in a small number of congregations, but soon became widespread. In 1980, Congress established the US Holocaust Memorial Council and provided for annual, national, civic commemoration of the Holocaust. The American inter-faith observance of Holocaust Remembrance Day is observed each year on 27 Nisan of the Jewish calendar, which falls on the fifth day following the eighth day of Passover. Others have suggested that Christians should include liturgical remembrance of the Shoah during Holy Week or, perhaps, on Passion Sunday.[5]

'The aim of Yom Hashoah,' writes Marcia Littell, who has collected together some of these liturgies, 'is not to place guilt or blame . . . but to help people of all faiths gain understanding of . . . an event in human history which speaks to the conscience of the world.'[5] In the same book, Alice Eckardt, recognizing that many of the perpetrators of the horrors were Christians, gives some important warnings to those arranging such services:[6]

1. Do not 'Christianize' the Holocaust.

2. Do not turn the Holocaust experience into a triumphalist demonstration of the truth of the Christian gospel.

3. Do not use readings from Jewish sources and then criticize, refute, or reinterpret them to fit Christian views.

4. Do not attempt to strip the Holocaust of its terrifying and awesome character.

5. Remember the total abandonment Jews experienced.

6. Finally, do not allow a Yom Hashoah service to become a one-time occurrence.[7]

Rabbi Albert Friedlander adds a further warning, if communal inter-faith services are envisaged and the initiative is taken by Christian communities, 'It must be remembered that the Holocaust continues to be the most sensitive area of contact between Jews and their neighbours. The local rabbi and members of the Jewish community must be included in the first planning sessions. This should start many months in advance – some problem always emerges which needs time to be resolved.'[8] He adds, however, the hope that, 'Remembering the past, praying for each other, we come to pray together. In that encounter, we encounter God.'[9]

The danger of confusion

Just as an ill-conceived Remembrance of the Holocaust might cause misunderstanding, so there is a danger that a Christian Seder may confuse the integrity of the two faith communities. The Seder ritual recalls the Passover and deliverance of the children of Israel from slavery in Egypt. It is very valuable for Christians to attend a Seder or Seder demonstration. The primary purpose of doing so should be to learn more about Judaism and to feel the Jewish sense of history and of joy in God's deliverance of his people. Christians are likely to become more aware of the close affinity of the two faiths and, particularly, to see how the eucharist grows out of the Passover ritual. Sometimes, however, the Seder is linked to a Christian communion. The danger of this is that it may serve to reinforce supersessionist theology, suggesting that the old covenant has been replaced by the new. It also imposes a Christian meaning on a Jewish ceremony, whereas the need is to try to understand the other faith in its integrity.

A witness to the future

With all the difficulties, inter-faith acts of witness, at their best, express and symbolize a vision of the underlying oneness of humankind's religious awareness and strengthen the sense of human unity.

There are a growing number of public occasions when people of different faiths wish to affirm values that they share. They may occur at the start of the Week of Prayer for World Peace, which is now observed in many countries, or on United Nations Day, with observances at the Cathedral of St John the Divine in New York and elsewhere, or on Commonwealth Day, which is marked by a multi-faith observance at Westminster Abbey, which is attended by the Queen or a member of the Royal Family. In Australia, there was a multi-faith ceremony when the new Houses of Parliament were opened at Canberra.

Usually, these occasions consist of readings and prayers from the different religions. The difficult issue, because it highlights the theological question of the relationship of religions, is whether there is anything that can be said or done together, such as joining in the universal prayer for peace or making joint affirmations.[10]

Is there a unity which transcends our particularity? This is the underlying suggestion of the inter-faith services arranged by the World Congress of Faiths. As Bishop George Appleton said in a sermon at such a service in 1970, 'We stand in worship before the Mystery of the Final reality to whom or to which we give different names, so great and deep and eternal, that we can never fully understand or grasp the mystery of His Being.'[11]

This is very challenging. Indeed a French psychologist who attended one of the conferences of the World Congress of Faiths, held in the early 1950s, said that inter-faith services would be the

most effective challenge to 'religious apartheid'. To share in them
affirms our recognition of one divine reality who transcends all our
particularities. It is to acknowledge that one God is known in all the
religious traditions of humankind. We may claim a special relationship with him or the fullest revelation, but in acknowledging
others we can learn from them and hope together to grow in our
religious understanding and faith.

We belong to particular religious communities, which we take
more or less seriously, just as we have our national identity with
which mostly we are content. Secure in this commitment, we can be
open to those of other faiths. At the start of the World Day of
Prayer for Peace at Assisi in October 1986, the Pope declared that
he was 'a believer in Jesus Christ, and in the Catholic Church, the
first witness of faith in him', but at once went on to say, 'It is, in fact,
my faith conviction which has made me turn to you.'[12]

Yet even more we need to recognize that we are children of one
God, who reveals himself in the covenant of Sinai and in Jesus
Christ and in all the religious traditions of humankind. When we
have discovered this, we are at home in any place of worship and
glad to worship together. We need to purge our theology and
practice of all that creates division and hostility and to recognize the
provisional nature of whatever path we follow. 'The function of a
religion,' writes John Hick, 'is to bring us to a right relationship with
the ultimate divine reality, to awareness of our true nature and our
place in the Whole, into the presence of God. In the eternal life
there is no longer any place for religions; the pilgrim has no need of
a way after he has finally arrived. In St John's vision of the heavenly
city at the end of our Christian scriptures it is said that there is no
temple – no Christian church or chapel, no Jewish synagogue, no
Hindu or Buddhist temple, no Muslim mosque, no Sikh
gurdwara . . . For all these exist in time, as ways through time to
eternity.'[13]

Long ago, a Sufi was on his way to the mosque and wrote in a
poem: 'Oh Lord, on my way to the mosque, I passed the Hindu
bowing to his idols and I wondered at how fervent he is in his
worship. Then I passed the Zoroastrian worshipping in front of his
fire, and I admired him for his zeal. Then I passed the Jewish
synagogue and I heard them reciting and I felt how pious the Jews
are. Then I passed the church and again the hymns were coming up
and I felt sympathy for them. Then I came to the mosque to worship

you. Then I wondered, and I said to myself, "how many are the different ways to you, the one and only God".'[14]

Jewish and Christian worship both point to a vision of a new world. For me, being together to pray is a symbolic expression of the relationship between peoples of different faiths for which I hope. Our human unity, of which the divine is the strongest guarantee, is affirmed, but our individuality, to which our particular faith traditions contribute, is acknowledged. As in prayer together we discover and celebrate our unity-in-diversity, we are given new resources to seek to reconcile the deep divisions in our world. For understanding between people of faith is a vital factor in the search for human peace and understanding.

> *Lord of all creation,*
> *we stand in awe before you,*
> *impelled by the visions of the harmony of all people.*
> *We are children of many traditions –*
> *inheritors of shared wisdom and tragic misunderstandings,*
> *of proud hopes and humble successes.*
> *Now it is time for us to meet –*
> *in memory and truth,*
> *in courage and trust,*
> *in love and promise.*
>
> *In that which we share,*
> *let us see the common prayer of humanity;*
> *in that in which we differ,*
> *let us wonder at the freedom of men and women;*
> *in our unity and our differences,*
> *let us know the uniqueness that is God.*[15]

14

Conclusion

From first meeting to being together to pray is a long journey. Jesus said, 'If you are about to offer your gift to God at the altar and there you remember that your brother has something against you, leave your gift there in front of the altar, go at once and make peace with your brother, and then come back and offer your gift to God' (Matt. 5.23–24).

Jews, justifiably, have much against Christians. The need to repent and seek reconciliation is necessary if Christians are to stand together with Jews in awe before the Lord of all creation. It is equally essential if Christian worship itself is to be authentic. The search for Christian–Jewish understanding is not just a matter of relations with Jews, but is vital to Christian wholeness – a wholeness which can only be rediscovered with Jewish help. If Christian practice and teaching bears part of the responsibility for the hideous suffering of Jews through the centuries and particularly during the Holocaust, then the credibility and integrity of Christianity itself is in question.

The changes made in official teaching have as yet only addressed the causes of offence; they have still to grapple with the rethinking and reformulation of central tenets of Christian belief. I hope I have indicated some of the areas where this rethinking and reformulation is necessary and possible forms that it might take.

A church which is open to the reality of Judaism will be a different and more humble church, but one, I believe, renewed in truth and holiness and more ready, in a suffering world, to share with others the love of God.

Notes

Introduction

1. Roger Hooker makes a similar point with reference to Hinduism in his recent *Themes in Hinduism and Christianity*, Verlag Peter Lang, Frankfurt 1989, e.g. on p. 4 and p. 13.

2. A phrase from Fred Kaan's hymn 'Lord, as we rise to leave the shell of worship' *100 Hymns for Today*, no. 52.

3. Fr Murray Rogers went to India in 1947 and after a time founded a Christian ashram at Jyotiniketan, near Bareilly. He and the community later moved to Jerusalem, then to Hong Kong and now to Canada. The words come from a conversation he had with me. The American professor James McClendon says that theology makes no sense detached from biography, and I recognize that my reflections are linked to personal experiences. See James William McClendon, Jr, *Biography as Theology*, Abingdon Press, Nashville and New York 1974.

4. See the introduction to my *Together to the Truth*, CLS, Madras 1971, pp. xi–xii.

5. John S. Dunne, *The Way of All the Earth*, Sheldon Press 1972, p. vii.

6. *CCJ Newsletter*, Autumn 1984.

7. *CCJ Newsletter*, Summer 1985.

8. Rt Rev David Sheppard, Bishop of Liverpool, in his Presidential Address to Liverpool Diocesan Synod on 11 March 1989, Cyclostyled text, p. 5.

9. Marc Ellis, *Toward a Jewish Theology of Liberation*, Orbis Books, Maryknoll 1987 and SCM Press 1988, p. 23.

10. So also Krister Stendahl, 'Judaism on Christianity: Christianity on Judaism', *Disputation and Dialogue*, ed. F. E. Talmage, Ktav, New York 1975, p. 337: 'It is clear to me that Christian theology needs a new departure. And it is equally clear that we cannot find it on our own, but only by the help of our Jewish colleagues.'

11. Johannes Baptist Metz, *The Emergent Church: The Future of Christianity in a Postbourgeois World*, Crossroad Publishing Co, New York and SCM Press 1981, p. 19.

12. See, for example, Choan-Seng Song, *The Compassionate God*, Orbis Books, Maryknoll and SCM Press 1982, passim, especially the Introduction, pp. 1–17.

13. See for example the writings of Earl Shorris or Roberta Strauss Feuerlicht to whom Marc Ellis refers, *Jewish Theology of Liberation* (n. 9), pp. 40–6.

14. See for example the criticisms made by the Oz VeShalom movement mentioned by Ellis, p. 56.

15. The reference is to a poem by the fourth-century mystical theologian Gregory Nazianzen, translated by Mary Rogers and quoted in *World Faiths Insight*, No. 99, Summer 1976, p. 20. Gregory Nazianzen's comments on the Jews are not fit to be quoted.

1. Roman Catholic Statements

1. *The Theology of the Churches and the Jewish People. Statements by the World Council of Churches and its Member Churches*, with a commentary by Allan

Brockway, Paul van Buren, Rolf Rendtorff, Simon Schoon, World Council of Churches, Geneva 1988 (= WCC), Preface, p. vii. There is a critical discussion of both WCC and Roman Catholic conceptions of inter-religious dialogue in Antonio Barbosa Da Silva, *Is There a New Imbalance in the Jewish–Christian Relationship?*, Department of Theology, Uppsala University, Sweden 1985.

2. Arthur Gilbert, *The Vatican Council and the Jews*, World Publishing Co, Cleveland 1968, p. 98. The book gives a good account of the various stages by which a declaration was agreed.

3. Quoted ibid., p. 98, from *Jewish Life*, New York, November–December 1963.

4. Quoted ibid., p. 126, from *Tradition*, New York, Fall 1964.

5. Gilbert, *Vatican Council and the Jews* (n. 2), p. 188.

6. Ibid., p. 197.

7. *Stepping Stones to Further Jewish–Christian Relations. An Unabridged Collection of Christian Documents*, compiled by Helga Croner, Stimulus Books, Paulist Press 1977, p. 1.

8. In *Stepping Stones* (n. 7), p. 11.

9. *The Common Bond. Notes on Preaching and Catechesis*, is reproduced, with accompanying articles, in SIDIC XIX, No. 2, Rome 1986, p. 13.

2. The World Council of Churches and Member Churches

1. Statement quoted in *Stepping Stones to Further Jewish–Christian Relations. An Unabridged Collection of Christian Documents*, compiled by Helga Croner, Stimulus Books, Paulist Press 1977, p. 7.

2. *The Theology of the Churches and the Jewish People. Statements by the World Council of Churches and its Member Churches*, with a commentary by Allan Brockway, Paul van Buren, Rolf Rendtorff, Simon Schoon, World Council of Churches, Geneva 1988, pp. 10f.

3. Quoted from *More Stepping Stones to Further Jewish–Christian Relations. An Unabridged Collection of Christian Documents 1975–1983*, compiled by Helga Croner, Stimulus Books, Paulist Press 1985, p. 163.

4. *The Theology of the Churches and the Jewish People* (n. 2), p. 37.

5. *World Council of Churches Consultation on the Church and the Jewish People: Sigtuna, Sweden, 30 October–4 November 1988, Report*, WCC, Geneva, p. 9.

6. 'Jews, Christians and Muslims: The Way of Dialogue', in *The Truth Shall Make You Free. The Lambeth Conference 1988*, Anglican Consultative Council, Appendix, p. 299. The sections on Judaism are reproduced in *Common Ground*, CCJ London, No. 4, 1988, p. 4.

7. *Anti-Semitism in the World Today*, Church of Scotland Board of World Mission and Unity 1985, Appendix VIII, p. 68.

8. *Christians and Jews Today*, Appendix VII, p. 55.

9. *Guidelines for Christian–Jewish Relations for Use in the Episcopal Church*, adopted and approved by the Presiding Bishop's committee on Christian–Jewish Relations, 27 October 1987 (cyclostyled), p. 3.

10. John Sargant, 'Review of *The Truth Shall Make You Free*', *World Faiths Insight* 23, October 1989, p. 48.

3. Is there a Consensus in the Churches?

1. *More Stepping Stones to Further Jewish–Christian Relations. An Unabridged Collection of Christian Documents 1975–1983*, compiled by Helga Croner, Stimulus Books, Paulist Press 1985, p. 208.

2. *The Truth Shall Make You Free. The Lambeth Conference 1988*, Anglican Consultative Council, p. 303.

3. *Common Ground*, CCJ, London 1989, No. 1, Kristallnacht Memorial Meeting.

4. *More Stepping Stones* (n. 1), p. 203.

5. Ibid., p. 213.

6. *The Theology of the Churches and the Jewish People. Statements by the World Council of Churches and its Member Churches*, with a commentary by Allan Brockway, Paul van Buren, Rolf Rendtorff, Simon Schoon, World Council of Churches, Geneva 1988, p. 164.

7. *The Common Bond. Notes on Preaching and Catechesis*, in SIDIC XIX, No. 2, Rome 1986, p. 25.

8. *The Theology of the Churches and the Jewish People* (n. 6), p. 184.

4. The Jewish Jesus

1. Alastair Hunter, 'Rite of Passage, the Implications of Matthew 4.1–11', *Christian–Jewish Relations*, Vol. 19 No. 4, December 1986, p. 8.

2. Early in this century Friedrich Delitzsch, the son of a noted Old Testament scholar, suggested Jesus was a Gentile. This was an isolated opinion, but late nineteenth-century writers ignored Jesus' Jewishness. Wellhausen's remark, early in this century, that Jesus was a Jew not a Christian, occasioned surprise. Occasionally at CCJ we received scurrilous anti-Jewish pamphlets claiming Jesus was a Gentile.

3. Marvin R. Wilson in *Our Father Abraham*, Eerdmans, Grand Rapids 1989, pp. 87–101, gives examples.

4. Günther Bornkamm, *Jesus of Nazareth*, Hodder & Stoughton and Harper & Row 1960; Ernst Fuchs, *Studies of the Historical Jesus*, SCM Press 1964.

5. Quoted in M. Braybrooke, *Together to the Truth*, CLS, Madras 1971, p. 81, from Vivekananda, *Christ the Messenger*, in *Selections from Swami Vivekananda*, Ramakrishna Mission Publications, Calcutta 1957. *Together to the Truth*, pp. 74–88, contains a discussion of the comments on Jesus made by leading figures in the Hindu renaissance.

6. See Pinchas Lapide and Hans Küng, *Brother or Lord?*, Fount Books 1977, pp. 13f. Schlom Ben-Chorim wrote *Jesus der Jude* in *Das Judentum in Ringen der Gegenwart*, Herbert Reich, Hamburg 1965.

7. Melito of Sardis, in 'The Homily on the Passion', in *Studies and Documents* 12, ed. C. Bonner, 1940, quoted by Marc Saperstein in *Moments of Crisis in Jewish–Christian Relations*, SCM Press and Trinity Press International 1989, p.6.

8. Quoted by Irving Greenberg in *Auschwitz: Beginning of An Era?*, ed. Eva Fleischner, Ktav, New York 1977, pp. 11f.

9. Quoted in Richard Rubenstein and John Roth, *Approaches to Auschwitz*, John Knox Press and SCM Press 1987, p. 309, from 'Ein Wort zur Judenfrage der Reichsbruderrat der Evangelischen Kirche in Deutschland', 8 April 1948, in *Der Ungekündigte Bund*, ed. Goldschmidt and Kraus, pp. 251–4.

10. See Saperstein, *Moments of Crisis* (n. 7), pp. 41f.

11. Luke 23.27 and 23.48. See E. Rivkin, *What Crucified Jesus?*, Abingdon Press, Nashville and SCM Press 1986.

12. E. Hoskyns, *We are the Pharisees*, reissued SPCK 1960.

13. Quoted by E. P. Sanders, *Jesus and Judaism*, SCM Press and Fortress Press, Philadelphia 1985, p. 18. See also Charlotte Klein, *Anti-Judaism in Christian Theology*, Fortress Press, Philadelphia 1978.

14. Wilson, *Our Father Abraham* (n. 3), p. 56.

15. John Riches, *Jesus and the Transformation of Judaism*, Darton, Longman and Todd 1980, p. 185, which otherwise is a valuable book.

16. Hans Conzelmann, *An Outline of the Theology of the New Testament*, SCM Press 1969, pp. 103f.

17. John Pawlikowski, *Christ in the Light of the Christian–Jewish Dialogue*,

Stimulus Books, Paulist Press, Ramsey, NJ 1982, p. 134 and pp. 89ff. See also Harvey Falk, *Jesus the Pharisee. A New Look at the Jewishness of Jesus*, Paulist Press, Mahwah, NJ 1985.

18. M. Hilton and G. Marshall. *The Gospels and Rabbinic Judaism: A Study Guide*, SCM Press and Ktav, New York 1988, p. 6.

19. Ibid., p. 35.

20. James H. Charlesworth, *Jesus Within Judaism*, SPCK 1989, passim.

21. See Raymond Brown, *The Community of the Beloved Disciple*, Geoffrey Chapman 1979.

22. *Hymns Ancient and Modern*, 210.

23. *Methodist Hymn Book*, 1933, No. 350.

24. E. P. Sanders, *Paul and Palestinian Judaism*, SCM Press and Fortress Press 1977, p. 59.

25. Ibid.

26. Pawlikowski, *Christ in the Light of the Christian–Jewish Dialogue* (n. 17), pp. 76–89. He refers particularly to the writings of Ellis Rivkin, e.g. *The Hidden Revolution: the Pharisees' Search for the Kingdom Within*, Abingdon Press, Nashville 1975. See also Hyam Maccoby, *Judaism in the First Century*, Sheldon Press 1989.

27. A good introduction to understanding the significance of Torah is to be found in Willem Zuidema, *God's Partner. An Encounter with Judaism*, SCM Press 1987, pp. 14–28.

28. John Bowker, *Jesus and the Pharisees*, Cambridge University Press 1973, p. 31. *Hakamim* is the term used by later rabbis to refer to their predecessors, and Bowker identifies them with the Pharisees.

29. See Pawlikowski, *Christ in the Light of the Christian–Jewish Dialogue* (n. 17), and the books by Jacob Neusner.

30. Sanders, *Jesus and Judaism* (n. 13), pp. 188ff.

31. Bowker, *Jesus and the Pharisees* (n. 28), p. 32.

32. Ibid., p. 38.

33. Wilson, *Our Father Abraham* (n. 3), pp. 64–72.

34. Brown, *Community of the Beloved Disciple* (n. 21).

35. Detailed arguments will be found in any critical Introduction to the New Testament, e.g. W. D. Davies, *Invitation to the New Testament*, SPCK 1967.

36. See Dennis Nineham's 'Epilogue' to *The Myth of God Incarnate*, ed. John Hick, SCM Press and Westminster Press, Philadelphia 1977.

37. Pawlikowski, *Christ in the Light of the Christian–Jewish Dialogue* (n. 17), pp. 92–3.

38. Bowker, *Jesus and the Pharisees* (n. 28), p. 32, and Sanders, *Jesus and Judaism* (n. 13), p. 206. See also Hilton and Marshall, *The Gospels and Rabbinic Judaism* (n. 18), pp. 17ff.

39. Bowker, *Jesus and the Pharisees* (n. 28), p. 44.

40. Sanders, *Jesus and Judaism* (n. 13), p. 210.

41. Ibid., p. 292. See also Michael Cook, 'Jesus and the Pharisees', *Journal of Ecumenical Studies* 15.3, 1978, pp. 132–47.

42. Sanders, *Jesus and Judaism* (n. 13), pp. 123ff.

43. For an account of the Essene community see Charlesworth, *Jesus Within Judaism* (n. 20), pp. 54–75, or G. Vermes, *The Dead Sea Scrolls in English*, Penguin Books (1962) [3]1987, pp. 1–57.

44. The Temple Scroll (11Q Temple 29, 8–10), see Sanders, *Jesus and Judaism* (n. 13), p. 85.

45. Matthew 19.28.

46. Isaiah 44.21.

47. Isaiah 56.6–8; Zechariah, 2.11; 8.20–22.

48. Sanders, *Jesus and Judaism* (n. 13), pp. 245ff.

49. Luke 24.21.

50. This has been the theme of the 'Parting of the Ways' Conferences organized by the Centre for the Study of Judaism and Jewish–Christian Relations, Birmingham, and CCJ. See Wilson, *Our Father Abraham* (n. 3), pp. 74–84.

51. Paul van Buren, quoted by Pawlikowski, *Christ in the Light of the Christian –Jewish Dialogue* (n. 17), p. 12.

52. *The Truth Shall Make You Free. The Lambeth Conference 1988*, Anglican Consultative Council, p. 300.

53. See Clark M. Williamson and Ronald J. Allen, *Interpreting Difficult Texts: Anti-Judaism and Christian Preaching*, SCM Press and Trinity Press International 1989.

5. *Questioning Christology*

1. Rosemary Ruether, 'Christology and Jewish–Christian Relations', In *Jews and Christians After the Holocaust*, ed. Abraham J. Peck, Fortress Press, Philadelphia 1982, p. 25.

2. Quoted by J. Schoneveld in *The Quarterly Review*, Vol. 4, No. 4, Winter 1984, from Friedrich-Wilhelm Marquardt, 'Feinde um unsretwillen; Das judische Nein und die christliche Theologie', *Treue zur Thora, Beiträge zur Mitte des christlich-judischen Gesprächs; Festschrift für Günther Harder zum 75 Geburtstag*, ed. Peter von der Osten-Sacken, Berlin, Institut Kirche und Judentum, [2]1979, p. 174.

3. See Larry W. Hurtado, *One God, One Lord*, Fortress Press, Philadelphia and SCM Press 1988.

4. Hans Conzelmann, *An Outline of the Theology of the New Testament*, SCM Press 1969, p. 140.

5. Quoted by John Pawlikowski, *Christ in the Light of the Christian–Jewish Dialogue*, Stimulus Books, Paulist Press, Ramsey, NJ 1982, p. 113, from Raymond Brown, 'Does the New Testament call Jesus God?', in *Theological Studies* 26, No. 4, Dec. 1965, p. 546.

6. Conzelmann, *Outline* (n. 4), p. 73.

7. Allan Brockway, *Learning Christology Through Dialogue With Jews*, WCC, Geneva 1985, p. 4.

8. *Hymns Ancient and Modern Revised* 51, verses 2, 7.

9. D. E. Nineham, *Saint Mark*, Penguin Books 1963, p. 227.

10. Ibid., pp. 398ff.

11. Conzelmann, *Outline* (n. 4), pp. 76–82.

12. Pawlikowski, *Christ in the Light of the Christian–Jewish Dialogue* (n. 5), p. 10. He refers in particular to the writings of the American Catholic Monika Hellwig.

13. Conzelmann, *Outline* (n. 4), p. 82.

14. Geza Vermes, *Jesus the Jew*, Fontana Books 1976, p. 186.

15. Conzelmann, *Outline* (n. 4), pp. 131–7. See also N. Perrin, *Rediscovering the Teaching of Jesus*, SCM Press 1967.

16. For a discussion see G. L. Prestige, *God in Patristic Thought*, SPCK 1959.

17. John Hick (ed.), *The Myth of God Incarnate*, SCM Press and Westminster Press, Philadelphia 1977, p. 178.

18. Gregory Baum, 'Catholic Dogma After Auschwitz', in *AntiSemitism and the Foundations of Christianity*, ed. Alan T. Davies, Paulist Press, New York 1979, p. 145.

19. Paul van Buren is writing a *Theology of the Jewish–Christian Reality*, Vol. I,

Discerning the Way, Seabury Press, New York 1980; Vol. II, *Christ in Context*, Harper and Row, San Francisco 1988. See also 'Jesus Christ as Shalom Between Jews and Christians', *Tantur Year Book*, Jerusalem 1984–5, pp. 129ff.

20. John Bowden, *Jesus: The Unanswered Questions*, SCM Press and Abingdon Press, Nashville 1988. p. 182, see also pp. 196–8.

21. D. M. Baillie, *God Was in Christ*, Faber 1961, pp. 106ff.

22. Pawlikowski's book gives several examples. See also Eugene B. Borowitz, *Contemporary Christologies: A Jewish Response*, Paulist Press 1980.

23. Alice L. Eckardt and A. Roy Eckardt, *Long Night's Journey Into Day*, Wayne State University Press, Detroit 1982, revd edn 1988, pp. 140f.

24. Pawlikowski, *Christ in the Light of the Christian–Jewish Dialogue* (n. 5), pp. 114–15.

25. Jacobus Schoneveld, 'The Jewish "No" to Jesus and the Christian "Yes" to Jews', *Quarterly Review* 4, 1984, p. 60, quoted by Alice and Roy Eckardt, *Long Night's Journey* (n. 23).

26. Rosemary Ruether, 'Old Problems and New Dimensions', in *AntiSemitism and the Foundations of Christianity*, (n. 18), p. 251.

27. Sydney Carter, 'Said Judas to Mary', *New Orbit*, ed. Peter Smith, Galliard 1972, No. 49.

28. Timothy Rees, 'O Crucified Redeemer', *100 Hymns for Today*, William Clowes and Sons 1969, No. 71.

6. An Eternal Covenant

1. *Nostra Aetate*, quoted in *Stepping Stones to Further Jewish–Christian Relations*, ed. Helga Croner, Stimulus Books 1977, pp. 1f.

2. *More Stepping Stones to Jewish Christian Relations*, ed. Helga Croner, Stimulus Books 1985, pp. 85f.

3. Ibid., p. 211.

4. Ibid., p. 186.

5. *The Truth Shall Make You Free. The Lambeth Conference 1988*, Anglican Consultative Council, pp. 302f.

6. Paul M. van Buren, *Discerning the Way*, Seabury Press, New York 1980, p. 42.

7. E. P. Sanders, *Jesus and Judaism*, SCM Press and Fortress Press 1985, p. 268.

8. W. D. Davies, 'From Schweitzer to Scholem: Reflections on Sabbatai Svi', *Journal of Biblical Literature*, 1976, p. 95.

9. E. P. Sanders, *Jesus and Judaism* (n. 7), p. 221.

10. John G. Gager, *The Origins of Anti-Semitism*, Oxford University Press 1983, p. 231. pp . 200f.

11. Ibid., p. 214.

12. Ibid., p. 215.

13. Ibid., p. 217.

14. K. Stendahl, 'The Apostle Paul and the Introspective Conscience of the West', *Harvard Theological Review* 56, 1963, pp. 199–215. Reprinted in *Paul Among Jews and Gentiles*, Fortress Press, Philadelphia and SCM Press 1976.

15. Gager, *Origins of Anti-Semitism* (n. 11), p. 223f.

16. Ibid., p. 260.

17. K. Stendahl, *Paul Among Jews and Gentiles* (n. 14), p. 4.

18. L. Gaston, *Paul and the Torah*, University of British Columbia Press, Vancouver 1987, p. 66.

19. Ibid., pp. 15–23 and passim.

20. E. P. Sanders, *Paul and Palestinian Judaism*, SCM Press and Fortress Press 1977, p. 551: 'Paul in fact explicitly denies that the Jewish covenant can be effective for salvation, thus consciously denying the basis of Judaism.'

21. See Marc Saperstein, *Moments of Crisis in Jewish–Christian Relations*, SCM Press and Trinity Press International 1989, pp. 2f. He quotes from Justin Martyr, *Dialogue with Trypho*, 47.1–4.

22. Terrence Callan, *Forgetting the Root: The Emergence of Christianity from Judaism*, Paulist Press 1986, passim.

23. Monika Hellwig, 'Christian Theology and the Covenant of Israel', *Journal of Ecumenical Studies* 7, Winter 1970, p. 49.

24. J. Pawlikowski, *Christ in the Light of the Christian–Jewish Dialogue*, Stimulus Books, Paulist Press, Ramsey, NJ 1982, pp. 2–35. Also, *What are they saying about Christian–Jewish Relations?*, Paulist Press 1980, pp. 33–68.

25. Paul M. van Buren, 'Christ of the church', paper presented to the American Academy of Religion Convention, San Francisco, December 1977, quoted by Pawlikowski, p. 13.

26. J. Coos Schoneveld, 'Israel and the Church in the Face of God: A Protestant Point of View', *Immanuel* 3, Winter 1973/74, pp. 80–3.

27. James Parkes, *Judaism and Christianity*, University of Chicago Press 1948, p. 30.

28. Pawlikowski, *Christ in the Light of the Jewish–Christian Dialogue* (n. 24), pp. 121f.

29. Ibid., p. 122.

30. Her position is summarized by Paul F. Knitter, *No Other Name?* Orbis Books, Maryknoll and SCM Press 1985, pp. 159ff.

31. Gerald H. Anderson, 'The Lordship of Jesus Christ and Religious Pluralism', in *Christ's Lordship and Religious Pluralism*, ed. G. H. Anderson and Thomas F. Stransky, Orbis Books, Maryknoll 1981, pp. 118–19.

7. God and Father of All

1. Wilfred Cantwell Smith, 'The Christian in a Religiously Plural World', in *Christianity and Other Religions*, ed. John Hick and Brian Hebblethwaite, Collins 1980, p. 87.

2. Ibid.

3. See *Can We Pray Together?*, British Council of Churches 1983, pp. 12f.

4. Eph. 1.20ff.; Col. 1.20.

5. See Kenneth Cracknell, *Towards a New Relationship*, Epworth Press 1986, especially pp. 70ff.

6. Quoted in Stephen Neill, *A History of Christian Missions*, Penguin Books 1964, p. 185.

7. See my 'Universalism', in *A New Dictionary of Christian Theology*, ed. Alan Richardson and John Bowden, SCM Press 1983, pp. 591f.

8. Bede Griffiths, *Christian Ashram*, Darton, Longman and Todd 1966, p. 194. See also my *The Undiscovered Christ*, CLS, Madras 1973.

9. Griffiths, *Christian Ashram*, (n. 8), p. 197.

10. Karl Rahner, *Theological Investigations*, Vol. 5, Darton, Longman and Todd 1966, p. 131.

11. See, for example, John Hick, *God and the Universe of Faiths*, Macmillan 1973; id. (ed.), *Truth and Dialogue*, Sheldon Press 1974; or id., 'Rethinking Christian Doctrine in the Light of Religious Pluralism', *IRF* (Newsletter of the International Religious Foundation), Vol. 3, No. 4, New York 1988.

See also R. Panikkar, 'Christianity and World Religions', *Christianity*, Punjabi University 1969, pp. 78ff. See also *Christian Revelation and World Religions*, ed. J. Neusner, Burns and Oates 1967.

12. M. M. Preminger, *The Sands of Tamanrasset: The Story of Charles de Foucauld*, London 1961, p. 55.

13. Kenneth Cragg, *Alive to God*, Oxford University Press 1970, p. 39.

14. See above, Chapter 5.

15. See above, Chapter 6, and *The Myth of Christian Uniqueness*, ed. John Hick, SCM Press and Westminster Press, Philadelphia 1977.

16. Dr Robert Runcie, 'Christianity and World Religions', *World Faiths Insight* 14, October 1986, p. 12.

17. George Appleton, 'Faiths in Fellowship', *World Faiths*, No. 101, Spring 1977, pp. 4f.

18. Robert Edward Whitson, *The Coming Convergence of World Religions*, Newman Press, Westminster, Md 1971, p. 185.

19. M. Hilton and G. Marshall, *The Gospels and Rabbinic Judaism*, SCM Press and Ktav, New York 1988, p. 154.

20. Kenneth Cragg, in his Preface to *Readings in the Qur'an*, Collins 1988, p. 9.

21. Rudolf Otto in *Religious Essays*, 1931.

22. See my article, 'Discovering Our Oneness as Servants of God', *World Faiths Insight*, New Series 15, February 1987, pp. 23–30.

23. C. F. Andrews, *What I Owe to Christ*, Hodder and Stoughton 1932, p. 153.

24. Schubert M. Ogden, *Christ Without Myth*, Collins 1962, p. 168.

8. Dialogue or Mission?

1. *Neve Shalom Newsletter*, 1983, quoted in *World Faiths Insight*, New Series 8, Jan. 1984, p. 35.

2. Diana L. Eck, 'What Do We Mean by "Dialogue"?', *Current Dialogue*, WCC, Geneva 1987, pp. 5ff.

3. See, for example, Muhammad Mashuq Ali's response to Professor Hans Küng's *Christianity and World Religions*, Collins 1987, in 'Christianity and World Religions: A Muslim Response', *World Faiths Insight*, New Series 22, Summer 1989, especially p. 6f.

4. See Paul Williams, 'Some Buddhist Reflections', *World Faiths Insight* 1989, pp. 13ff.

5. Rabbi Dr Norman Solomon, 'Jewish/Christian Dialogue. The State of the Art', *Studies in Jewish/Christian Relations*, No. 1, Selly Oak, Birmingham 1984, p. 8.

6. Eugene R. Borowitz, *Contemporary Christologies: A Jewish Response*, Paulist Press 1980, p. 19, see also p. 7.

7. Rabbi Rodney Mariner, 'A Jewish Response to Christian Missionary Activity', an unpublished paper given to the CCJ Missionary Advisory Committee, p. 1. Haman, in the book of Esther, tries to persuade King Ahasuerus to kill all the Jews.

8. Allan Brockway, *The Theology of the Churches and the Jewish People*, WCC, Geneva 1988, p. 124. Christian missionaries believed that what they were doing was for the good of Jews and their eternal salvation.

9. Ibid., p. 125.

10. Ibid., p. 128, quoting from WCC archives.

11. See above, p. 31.

12. Statement of the CCJ Executive, March 1986.

13. Dr Robert Runcie, 'Christianity and World Religions', *World Faiths Insight*, No. 14, Oct. 1986, p. 13.

14. Donald Coggan, *When Christian meets Jew*, 1985 St Paul's Lecture, London Diocesan Council for Christian–Jewish Understanding, pp. 6f.

15. Ibid., p. 8.

16. Mariner, 'Jewish Response' (n. 7), p. 3.

17. See my article 'Jesus as Others See Him', *Modern Churchman*, 1988, New Series XXX No. 1, p. 1. Although 'syncretism' is usually used in a pejorative sense, Michael Pye in the article in the *New Dictionary of Christian Theology*, ed. Alan Richardson

and John Bowden, SCM Press 1983, quotes J. Kamstra, 'To be human is to be syncretist'.

18. John Dunne, *The Way of All the Earth*, Sheldon Press 1972, Preface. See the Introduction, above p. 2.

19. Mariner, 'Jewish Response' (n. 7); see also Rabbi Dr N. Solomon, 'Judaism and World Religions', *World Faiths Insight*, New Series 12, February 1986, and Ze'ev W. Falk, 'From East to West My Name is Lauded Among the Nations', in *The Experience of Religious Diversity*, ed. John Hick and Hasan Askari, Gower 1985, pp. 25ff.

20. See especially *The Myth of Christian Uniqueness*, ed. John Hick and Paul Knitter, Orbis Books, Maryknoll and SCM Press 1988.

21. See note 15 to the Introduction.

9. Shoah

1. See the papers presented at the Conference 'Remembering for the Future' at Oxford in 1988, published by Pergamon Press 1988.

2. Alice L. Eckardt and A. Roy Eckardt, *Long Night's Journey Into Day*, Wayne State University Press, Detroit 1982 revd edn 1988, p. 54.

3. Ibid.

4. Enda McDonaugh at the ICCJ Colloquium, Dublin 1985.

5. Eliezer Berkovits, *Faith After the Holocaust*, Ktav, New York 1973, quoted by W. Zuidema, *God's Partner. An Encounter with Judaism*, SCM Press 1987, p. 204. Arthur A. Cohen explained in *The Tremendum*, Crossroad Publishing Company, New York 1987, that earlier he 'had no language with which to speak of the evil'.

6. Yehuda Amichai, in his novel *Not of This Time, Not of this Place*, quoted in *Auschwitz: Beginning of a New Era? Reflection on the Holocaust*, ed. E. Fleischner, Ktav, New York 1977, p. ix.

7. Elie Wiesel's Foreword to *Jews and Christians After the Holocaust*, ed. Abraham J. Peck, Fortress Press, Philadelphia, 1982, p. xi.

8. Michael Berenbaum, 'The Uniqueness and Universality of the Holocaust', *Christianity and Judaism: The Deepening Dialogue*, ed. Richard W. Rousseau SJ, Ridge Row Press, University of Scranton, Pa. 1983, p. 83.

9. There is a valuable discussion in Marc Saperstein, *Moments of Crisis in Jewish–Christian Relations*, SCM Press and Trinity Press International 1989, pp. 45–50.

10. *The Scribe. Journal of Babylonian Jewry*, No. 18, March 1986.

11. The similarities between early and mediaeval church law and Nazi legislation are detailed by Raul Hilberg in *The Destruction of European Jews*, Harper and Row, New York 1961. Examples of his work are quoted by Marc Ellis, *Toward a Jewish Theology of Liberation*, Orbis Books, Maryknoll 1987 and SCM Press 1988, pp. 123–5.

12. Martin Gilbert, *The Holocaust*, Weidenfeld and Nicolson 1985, p. 1.

13. See Choan Seng Song, *The Compassionate God*, Orbis Books, Maryknoll and SCM Press 1982, pp. 12–14 and passim. This is also pointed out in the writings of Rosemary Ruether, see her 'Feminism and Jewish–Christian Dialogue', in *The Myth of Christian Uniqueness*, ed. John Hick and Paul F. Knitter, Orbis Books, Maryknoll and SCM Press 1987, pp. 137–48.

14. Cited by Franklin H. Littell in his Foreword to *Exile in the Fatherland: Martin Niemöller's Letters from Moabit Prison*, ed. Hubert G. Locke, Eerdmans, Grand Rapids 1986.

15. See Marc Saperstein, *Toward a Jewish Theology of Liberation* (n. 11), pp. 45–8.

16. The use of 'old' and 'new' of covenant, testament or people of God is best avoided, because it carries with it, especially to Jewish ears, the implication that the

church has replaced the Jewish people and that God abandoned them because they killed Jesus.

17. See Marvin Wilson, *Our Father Abraham*, Eerdmans, Grand Rapids 1989, pp. 87–101.

18. Quoted by Gill Seidel, *The Holocaust Denial. Beyond the Pale Collective*, Leeds 1986, p. 68. See also, for example, *Holocaust News*, The Centre for Historical Review, PO. Box 446.

19. Alan Ecclestone, *The Night Sky of the Lord*, Darton, Longman and Todd 1980, p. 24.

20. The Revd Canon Dr Anthony Phillips, 'Why the Jews Should Forgive', *The Times*, 8 June 1985. His article and Albert Friedlander's, together with other comments, are reproduced in *European Judaism*, 1985, 2.

21. Ibid.

22. Rabbi Dr Albert Friedlander, 'The Holocaust Must Not Be Forgotten', *The Times*, 4 May 1985.

23. Eugene Heimler, 'Forty Years On', *Manna*, No. 8, Summer 1985, p. 2.

24. Albert Friedlander, 'Judaism and the Concept of Forgiving', *Christian Jewish Relations*, Vol. 19, No. 1, March 1986, p. 9.

25. Rabbi A. Bayfield, *Remembrance and Forgiveness*, Lecture to Holy Blossom Temple, Toronto, 11 November 1987.

26. Friedlander, 'Judaism' (n. 24), p. 9.

27. Quoted by Cynthia Ozick in Simon Wiesenthal's *The Sunflower*, New York 1973, p. 186.

28. Bayfield, *Remembrance* (n. 25), p. 8.

29. Ibid.

30. *Jewish Encylopaedia*, 'Forgiveness'.

31. Maimonides, *Mishneh Torah, Hilchot Teshuvah II*.

32. Bayfield, *Remembrance* (n. 25), p. 13.

33. Friedlander, 'Judaism' (n. 24), p. 8.

34. Anthony Phillips, 'Forgiveness Reconsidered', *Christian–Jewish Relations*, Vol. 19, No. 1, p. 17, quoting from *Common Ground*, CCJ, London, XXII.3, 1968, p. 4.

35. Friedlander, 'Judaism' (n. 24), p. 8.

36. Michael Goldberg, *Namesake*, Yale University Press 1980, p. 87.

37. Kenneth E. Kirk, *Some Principles of Moral Theology*, London 1920, p. 170.

38. Phillips, 'Forgiveness Reconsidered' (n. 34), p. 15.

39. 'Amazing Grace', by John Newton, in *Combined Sound of Living Waters and Fresh Sounds*, Hodder and Stoughton 1977, p. 15.

40. Dorothy Sayers, *Unpopular Opinions. Twenty-One Essays*, London 1951.

41. See my article on 'Universalism', in *A New Dictionary of Christian Theology*, ed. Alan Richardson and John Bowden, SCM Press 1983.

42. Friedlander, 'Judaism' (n. 24), p. 10.

43. Phillips, 'Why the Jews Should Forgive' (n. 20).

44. Rabbi Hugo Gryn, 'Creative Suffering: A Jewish View', *World Faiths*, No. 110, Spring 1980, p. 22.

45. Albert Friedlander, *Against the Fall of Night*, 1984 Waley Cohen Lecture, CCJ, p. 5.

46. Bayfield, *Remembrance* (n. 24), p. 24.

10. Faith after Auschwitz

1. Johann-Baptist Metz, *Christen und Juden nach Auschwitz*, Munich/Mainz 1980.

2. Clifford Longley, 'Insular Vision of the Holocaust', *The Times*, 4 March 1985. See also *Concilium*, October 1984.

Notes

173

3. Rabbi Dr Norman Solomon, *Jewish Responses to the Holocaust*, Centre for the Study of Judaism and Jewish Christian Relations, Selly Oak Colleges, Birmingham 1988. p. 7. See also Dan Cohn-Sherbok, 'Jewish Theology and the Holocaust', *Theology*, Vol. 86, March 1983, p. 84.

4. E. Fackenheim, *The Unconquerable Spirit*, Mesorah, New York 1980, pp. 27f. See also Solomon, the *Jewish Reponses* (n. 3), pp. 7–9, for the reference to E. Wasserman.

5. Quoted by Alice L. Eckardt and A. Roy Eckardt,, *Long Night's Journey Into Day*, Wayne State University Press, 1982, pp. 80–2.

6. Richard Rubenstein, *After Auschwitz*, Bobbs-Merrill, Indianapolis 1968, pp. 128f.

7. Elie Wiesel, *Night*, Orbis Books, Maryknoll 1987 and SCM Press 1988, see also Marc H. Ellis, *Toward a Jewish Theology of Liberation*, pp. 7–24.

8. E. Fackenheim, in *Christian Century*, 29 July 1970, p. 923.

9. E. Fackenheim, 'Jewish Faith and the Holocaust', *Commentary*, XLV, 2, Summer 1969.

10. E. Fackenheim, 'Jewish Values in the Post-Holocaust Future', *Judaism*, XV.3, Summer 1969.

11. Irving Greenberg, 'Theological Reflections on the Holocaust', in Eva Fleischner (ed.), *Auschwitz: Beginning of a New Era?*, Ktav, New York 1977, p. 32.

12. Ibid., p. 30.

13. E. Berkovits, *Faith After the Holocaust*, Ktav, New York 1973. See Cohn-Sherbok, 'Jewish Theology' (n. 3).

14. Greenberg, 'Theological Reflections' (n. 11), p. 27.

15. Ibid., pp. 27f.

16. Rabbi A. Lelyveld, *Atheism is Dead*, World Publishing Co., New York 1968, quoted by Eckardts, *Long Night's Journey* (n. 5), p. 86.

17. Ibid., pp. 86f.

18. E. Berkovits, *Faith After the Holocaust*, Ktav, New York 1973, quoted by Eckardts, *Long Night's Journey* (n. 5), p. 90.

19. I. Maybaum, *The Face of God After Auschwitz*, Polak and Van Gennep Ltd, 1965. p. 84.

20. Quoted by Francis House in *Theology* LXXXIII, November 1980, pp. 409ff.

21. Jürgen Moltmann, *The Crucified God*, SCM Press and Harper and Row 1978, p. 278. See also, id., *The Experiment Hope*, Fortress Press, Philadelphia and SCM Press 1975.

22. Rabbi Dr Albert Friedlander, *Against the Fall of Night*, 1984 Waley Cohen Lecture, CCJ, p. 5.

23. Peter von der Osten Sacken, *Grundzüge einer Theologie im Christlich–jüdischem Gespräch* (1982). pp. 18f.; his italics. The quotations are from Clement Thoma's *Christliche Theologie des Judentums*, 1978, pp. 242ff. and Franz Mussner's *Traktat über die Juden*, 1979, pp. 77ff. Quoted by Albert Friedlander, *Against the Fall* (n. 22), p. 6.

24. Mussner, p. 78. See previous note.

25. A full critique of Moltmann's position is made by the Eckhardts, *Long Night's Journey* (n. 5), pp. 114ff.

26. G. Baum, *Man Becoming: God in Secular Experience*, Herder and Herder 1971, quoted by the Eckardts, *Long Night's Journey* (n. 5), pp. 83f.

27. C. E. Rolt, *The World's Redemption*, 1913, p. 185.

28. W. H. Vanstone, *Love's Endeavour, Love's Expense*, Darton, Longman and Todd 1977, p. 51.

29. Hans Jonas, 'The Concept of God after Auschwitz', reprinted from *Harvard Theological Review*, Vol. 55, 1962, pp. 1–20, in *Out of the Whirlwind*, ed.

A. Friedlander, Schocken Books, New York 1976, pp. 465–476, here pp. 465f. Also included in Hans Jonas, *The Phenomenon of Life: Toward a Philosophical Biology*, Harper and Row, New York 1966.

30. Dorothee Sölle, 'God's Pain and Our Pain: How Theology has to Change after Auschwitz', Pre-papers for *Remembering the Future*, Pergamon Press 1988, Supplementary volume, p. 454.

11. Israel

1. Conor Cruise O'Brien, *The Siege*, Weidenfeld and Nicolson 1986, pp. 30f.

2. Marc Ellis, *Toward a Jewish Theology of Liberation*, Orbis Books 1987 and SCM Press 1988, pp. 37f. He quotes from Nathan Perlmutter and Ruth Ann Perlmutter, *The Real Anti-Semitism in America*, Arbor House, New York 1982, p. 107.

3. 'Christians and Jews Today', Appendix VII to *Board of World Mission and Unity Report to the General Assembly of the Church of Scotland*, 1985, p. 56.

4. Statement of the General Assembly of the Presbyterian Church (USA) in *The Theology of the Churches and the Jewish People*, WCC, Geneva 1988, p. 117.

5. Peter Schneider, *The Christian Debate on Israel*, The Centre for the Study of Judaism and Jewish Christian Relations, Selly Oak Colleges, Birmingham, n.d. p. 28.

6. Henry Siegman, 'A Decade of Catholic–Jewish Relations – A Reassessment', *Journal of Ecumenical Studies*, 15, 1978, p. 252.

7. The Pittsburg Platform. Text in full in *Encyclopaedia Judaica*, XIII pp. 570–1.

8. Uri Davis, however, for example, is very critical of Zionism. See his *Israel: Utopia Incorporated*, Zed Books 1977, p. 13: 'It is in the effort to disguise the concrete context of the emergence of the Zionist movement that the Israeli–Jewish obsession with archeology, a desperate attempt to legitimize the endeavour in terms of ruins 2000 years old, is rooted. Similarly, the consistent avoidance of dealing with the era of the crusades; the compulsion to obliterate all physical remains of the dispossessed Palestinian–Arab native peasant population (385 Arab villages have been destroyed and razed to the ground within pre-1967 Israel proper); the reification of anti-Semitic racism as an objective immutable, inherent characteristic of non-Jewish human nature; the militarization of the Old Testament, and finally, the elimination by fiat of 2000 years of the country's history and the seeking of justification not in terms of its concrete reality but in genocidal conquest of the land by a Hebrew criminal, elevated to the position of national hero: Joshua son of Nun. How else could the Zionist endeavour be justified in terms of the concrete reality of Palestine, a country under Ottoman occupation with a native peasantry living under conditions of feudal tenancy and serfdom?' A Christian who takes a hostile view of Zionism is Andrew Kirk, 'The Middle East Dilemma: A Personal Reflection', *Anvil*, Vol. 3, No. 3, 1986.

9. For the continuity of Jewish links with the Land and of a Jewish presence there see, for example, Chaim Seidler-Feller, 'The Land of Israel: Sanctified Matter or Mythic Space', in *Three Faiths – One God*, ed. John Hick and Edmund S. Meltzer, Macmillan 1989, pp. 137–64; Tudor Parfitt, 'The Jewish Presence in Jerusalem 1800–1881', *Jerusalem Perspectives*, ed. Peter Schneider and Geoffrey Wigoder, London Rainbow Group 1976, pp. 5–10. The whole booklet is useful: *Jerusalem*, Israel Pocket Library, Keter Publishing House, Jerusalem 1973, pp. 38–143, extracted from the *Encyclopaedia Judaica*.

10. Michael Palumbo, *The Palestinian Catastrophe*, Faber and Faber 1987, pp. 206f.

11. See the discussion on 'Empowerment' in Marc Ellis, *Toward a Jewish Theology* (n. 2), pp. 25–39.

12. Irving Greenberg, 'The Third Great Cycle in Jewish History', in *Perspectives*, National Jewish Resource Centre, New York 1981, p. 18.

13. Palumbo, *Palestinian Catastrophe* (n. 10), passim.

14. Conor Cruise O'Brien, *The Siege* (n. 1), p. 34. References, unless otherwise stated, are to this book.

15. Theodor Herzl, *Zionist Writings and Addresses*, pp. 112 and 114.

16. L. Stein, *The Balfour Declaration*, Vallentine Mitchell 1961, p. 526.

17. Balfour Declaration, 2 November 1917.

18. Report to the Foreign Office by Sir Gilbert Clayton, quoted D. Ingrams, *Seeds of Conflict*, John Murray 1972, pp. 43f.

19. J. Bowle, *Viscount Samuel*, Gollancz 1957, p. 191.

20. B. Wassertein, *The British in Palestine*, Royal Historical Society 1979, p. 48.

21. Ibid., p. 107.

22. Conor Cruise O'Brien, *The Siege* (n. 1), p. 175.

23. Ibid., p. 238.

24. K. Harris, *Attlee*, Weidenfeld and Nicolson 1982, p. 390.

25. See Conor Cruise O'Brien, *The Siege* (n. 1), pp. 417f.

26. Ibid.

27. Ibid., p. 578.

28. I. Rabinovich, *The War for Lebanon*, Cornell University Press, Ithaca, NY 1984, p. 149.

29. Government Press Office, 15 September, quoted Conor Cruise O'Brien, *The Siege* (n. 1), p. 629.

30. Quoted Conor Cruise O'Brien, *The Siege* (n. 1), p. 634.

31. Ellis, *Toward a Jewish Theology* (n. 2), pp. 55–8.

32. A good account of those Christians who have suported the return of the Jews to the Land of Israel is given by Michael J. Pragai, *Faith and Fulfilment*, Vallentine Mitchell 1985.

33. Statement of Christian leaders: Revd Alfred Sawyer and others, cyclostyled summer 1989.

34. See *Nes Ammim News,* Doar Na Ashrat, Israel, Summer 1988.

35. Statement of the General Assembly of the Presbyterian Church (USA) (n. 4).

36. See for example the Christian Aid video, *Palestine: Much Promised Land*.

37. Interviewed in *Unified in Hope*, ed. Carolin J. Birkland, WCC, Geneva 1987, p. 19.

38. Ibid., p. 106.

39. Ysuf al-Khal, *Al-B'ir al-Mahjurah*, 'The Abandoned Well', *Collected Poems*, Dar Majallat Sha'ir, Beirut, n.d. quoted by Kenneth Cragg, *This Year in Jerusalem*, Darton, Longman and Todd 1982, p. 88.

40. Kamal Nasir, *Jirah Tughanni*, Dar al-Tali'ah, Beirut 1960, p. 197, quoted by Kenneth Cragg, p. 60.

12. A Shared Responsibility

1. Quoted in A. Peacock's *Fellowship Through Religion*, World Congress of Faiths 1956, p. 21.

2. *Common Ground*, No. 3, 1987. It must be admitted that to date there is no particular evidence that anyone has responded to this 'urging'.

3. Sir Immanuel Jakobovits, *From Doom to Hope*, Office of the Chief Rabbi, January 1986, p. 5.

4. Ibid., p. 9. For a critical response, see, for example, Edie Friedman, '*Faith in the City*: An Alternative Jewish view', *The Jewish Quarterly*, Vol. 33. No. 3, 1986, pp. 20–5.

5. Sir Immanuel Jakobovits, *Aids, Jewish Perspectives*, Office of the Chief Rabbi 1987.

6. David J. Goldberg, 'Not to Mock, Lament, or Execrate, but Understand', *The Independent*, 10 October 1987.

7. H. Küng, 'No Peace in the World without Peace among Religions', *World Faiths Insight*, New Series 21, February 1989, p. 14.

8. David Jenkins, *What is Man?*, SCM Press Press 1970; Michael Ramsey, *The Glory of God and the Transfiguration of Christ*, Longmans 1949.

9. *Values and Social Change in Britain*, ed. Mark Abrams, David Gerard and Noel Tims, Macmillan 1985, p. 16.

13. Together to Pray

1. Leaflet of the All-Faiths Chapel of the Universalist Church of New York City at Central Park, to which I was taken in the early 1970s by my friend the late Roland Gammon. He writes about the chapel in his *Nirvana Now*, World Authors Ltd, New York 1980, pp. 337–9 and p. 536. I think these are words of Evelyn Underhill, but I cannot trace the source. They reflect her views in, for example, *The Mystic Way*, J. M. Dent, London 1913, pp. 3–57. In his sermon to the World Congress of Faiths 1967 Conference, Bishop Hugh Montefiore said, 'We all meet in the one God', quoted in *Inter-Faith Worship*, ed. Marcus Braybrooke, Galliard, Stainer and Bell, 1974, p. 8.

2. Krister Stendahl, 'Judaism on Christianity: Christianity on Judaism', *Disputation and Dialogue, Readings in Jewish–Christian Encounter*, ed. F. E. Talmage, Ktav, New York 1975, pp. 333f. There is a useful discussion of these issues in Clark M. Williamson and Ronald J. Allen, *Interpreting Difficult Texts: Anti- Judaism and Christian Preaching*, SCM Press and Trinity Press International 1989. The Lambeth Conference spoke of 'the profound changes and potential for good in modern scholarly understanding of the Bible', *The Truth Shall Make you Free. The Lambeth Conference 1988*, Anglican Consultative Council, p. 300 or *Common Ground*, CCJ, No. 4, 1988, p. 5.

3. See my 'Jesus who Unites and Divides', *Discernment*, Vol. 1, No. 3, Winter 1986/7, pp. 31–3.

4. See my 'Praying Together: Possibilities and Difficulties of Interfaith Worship', *Dialogue and Alliance*, Vol. 3, No. 1, Spring 1989, p. 89–93.

5. Albert Friedlander, in *The Six Days of Destruction*, by E. Wiesel and A. Friedlander, Pergamon Press 1988, pp. 59–61.

6. Marcia Littell, *Liturgies on the Holocaust*, The Edwin Mellen Press, Lewiston, NY and Queenston, Ontario 1986, p. 7.

7. Ibid., pp. 11–17.

8. Friedlander, *Six Days* (n.4), p. 60.

9. Ibid., p. 61.

10. *Dialogue and Alliance*, (n. 4), pp. 91f.

11. Bishop George Appleton in a sermon preached at King's College, London, quoted in *Inter-Faith Worship* (n. 1), p. 8.

12. Pope John Paul II at the World Day of Prayer for Peace in Assisi, 27 October 1986: *Osservatore Romano*, printed also in *World Faiths Insight*, New Series 15, February 1987, p. 3.

13. John Hick, *God and the Universe of Faiths*, Macmillan 1973, p. 147.

14. Quoted by Dr Zaki Badawi, 'Islam and the Language of Dialogue', *World Faiths Insight*, New Series 17, October 1987, p. 21.

15. Quoted in *Prayers for Peace*, selected by Robert Runcie and Basil Hume, SPCK 1987, p. 21, taken from *Forms of Prayer for Jewish Worship: Daily, Sabbath and Occasional Prayers*, Reform Synagogues of Great Britain, [7]1977.

Bibliography

Those who wish to pursue the issues raised will find a full bibliography on Christian–Jewish relations in Kenneth Cracknell's *Towards a New Relationship*, Epworth Press 1986.

A few books are listed below.

Church statements

Stepping Stones to Further Jewish–Christian Relations and *More Stepping Stones to Jewish–Christian Relations*, compiled by Helga Croner, Stimulus Books, Paulist Press 1977 and 1985

The Theology of the Churches and the Jewish People, WCC, Geneva 1988

On Judaism, Jesus and christology

E. P. Sanders, *Jesus and Judaism* and *Paul and Palestinian Judaism*, SCM Press and Fortress Press 1985 and 1977

John Pawlikowski, *Christ in the Light of Christian–Jewish Dialogue*, Stimulus Books, Paulist Press 1982

Willem Zuidema, *God's Partner*, SCM Press 1987

Hyam Maccoby, *Judaism in the First Century*, Sheldon Press 1988

The Myth of God Incarnate, ed. John Hick, SCM Press and Westminster Press 1977

On the theology of religions:

The Myth of Christian Uniqueness, ed. John Hick, Orbis Books and SCM Press 1988

Paul F. Knitter, *No Other Name*, Orbis Books and SCM Press 1985

The Holocaust

Approaches to Auschwitz, ed. Richard L. Rubinstein and John K. Roth, John Knox Press and SCM Press 1987

Out of the Whirlwind, ed. Albert Friedlander, Schocken Books 1976

Dan Cohn-Sherbok, *Holocaust Theology*, Lamp Press 1989

Israel

For the history, Conor Cruise O'Brien, *The Siege*, Weidenfeld and Nicolson, 1985

Kenneth Cragg, *This Year in Jerusalem*, Darton, Longman and Todd 1982

Index